THE THERAPIST FROM ANOTHER WORLD:
Clinical Vignettes from Homebased Counseling, AIDS Awareness Prevention, Anger Management... and More!

by

Bo Wilson

DORRANCE
PUBLISHING CO
EST. 1920
PITTSBURGH, PENNSYLVANIA 15238

Dorrance Publishing Co
585 Alpha Drive
Suite 103
Pittsburgh, PA 15238
Visit our website at *www.dorrancebookstore.com*

ISBN: 978-1-6393-7228-7
eISBN: 978-1-6393-7630-8

INTRODUCTION

Since this is my first book, I figured, why not begin with a bit of a jolt?

While working at one of my earlier jobs, as a milieu therapist in a psychiatric hospital, I had four days off. One night I had the most horrific dream of my life. The psychiatric unit was located on the second floor of a separate building from the rest of the hospital. In my dream, as I approach the elevator I happen to look into the four-inch space between the elevator and adjoining wall. Crushed and wedged in this space was the body of a young male. Not knowing what to do, I began to panic and tremble. The thought I had (in the dream) was that I had to do something! At least get the body out. But how? So I figured that I'd get a crowbar, swing it, hook the body, and yank it out. Then I thought that the body would come out in chunks, bloody and rotten. Nice dream, huh? So, now I'm crying and really shaking.

I woke up with my first panic attack. My heart was pounding, and I was drenched in sweat. And immediately thinking: "What a fucked-up dream!" and I'm wondering where it came from. So I lay in bed and did some crisis-dream analysis. Started with Freudian…nah… made no sense. Moved on to Gestalt interpretation. Projection and closure… figure/background. I was working in inpatient with suicidal and psychotic individuals. I had my own stressors. So this was probably a combination of multiple factors and my neurons blasting away during deep REM sleep. Right? But I was really struck by how freaked out I was, the somatic reactions and feelings of despair. Looking back, I realized it was like PTSD.

So I returned to work on Monday and was sitting in the nurses' station writing progress notes. Sixteen-year-old Sarah comes in to shoot the breeze. She says, "So you have been off for several days."

I said, "Yup."

Sarah continues with, "The new patient freaked out in group; her son recently died. Fell down an elevator shaft and got wedged between the elevator and the wall. Was really struck and they had trouble getting his body out." Cue the *Twilight Zone* theme!

I believe that I had a premonitory dream. When I'd left for my four-day vacation, I had known nothing of this patient or her situation. Pretty weird stuff!

While writing this book, I've read excerpts to family, friends, and other clinicians. The most frequent response has been "Did that really happen?" None of what you are about to read is fictional or dramatized. I've been writing case studies and workshops for thirty years. I've saved all my progress notes. When I went on my yearly vacation to Jamaica, I had a system. Two or three days of nothing work related. Then I would write every morning or afternoon. Individual case studies, family systems theory, holistic techniques, foster family therapy sessions, addiction, HIV, anger management, explosive adolescent girls, and on and on. I always felt like I needed to get away from the daily clinical work to be able to recharge and write in as an objective way as possible. People thought I was slightly nuts. I mean, vacation time spent working?

But when I returned from vacation, I would be recharged and have new workshops, vignettes, and case studies. And my clients absolutely loved these stories. The crazier the better! Adults, kids, anger-management groups, DYS residents, young moms. They all loved these stories. I know it's the drama and humor and entertainment value. Clients and clinicians and friends and family have been saying "You gotta write a book" for twenty years. I would be like "Yeah, yeah, yeah," but the thought was daunting.

But the more I shared clinical stories with other therapists, the more I realized that my clinical world was radically different from their experiences. Except for other home-based counselors who worked with multi-problem families. And the professional journals would often frustrate the hell out of me. One-dimensional treatment. No systemic or holistic points of view. Little consideration for the effects of chronic substance abuse, domestic violence, and gender bias. And over reliance on meds. I would read a case study and think, "It's so much more complicated." Managed care mentally also drove me nuts. Little attention given to the process of gaining trust than natural progression of a therapeutic relationship, family and systemic homeostasis, treatment regression, individual maturation, and second-order change.

When I worked in inpatient psychiatry, first-order change or symptom reduction were the goals. Medicate, stabilize with 1:1 (one on one) counseling or group, and return the patient to an unchanged family system that perpetuated the pathology. And on some level, everybody knew it. It was called the Band-Aid approach, and everyone just shrugged. I worked in three different hospitals with multiple psychiatrists who had varying diagnostic criteria and different meds. One hospital viewed confused patients as falling into the schizophrenia realm. Another saw the same individuals as within the bipolar spectrum. Same patients, same symptoms, different diagnoses, different meds. Minimal attention paid to substance use or family issues. The recidivism rate was through the roof. Gee, what a shock.

So, thirty years ago, to be better able to facilitate second-order change, I decided to see all my clients in their natural setting, with the exceptions of anger management and prevention programs. I also decided not to utilize insurance and base my fees on the distance I drove and the length of sessions. I mixed modalities of treatment, based on what needed to be addressed. I felt that self-pay made everyone more accountable. I wouldn't get paid unless my clients felt the services were productive. And they wouldn't just hand over an insurance card. And the insurance company couldn't dictate the type, length, or frequency of treatment. A contract between myself and my clients. I would use traditional diagnoses, but I would also empower, educate, normalize, and reframe symptoms using a holistic, systemic, feministic, and ego-supportive point of view. Just made sense to me!

I've had (and still have) clients for over twenty years. Some of them I see or talk to once a month or two or three times per year. I also have clients that I am working with the third generation. Mother/grandmother, son/dad, and daughter/granddaughter. By the way, you know you're getting old when your new client's grandmother is five years younger than you are. But the treatment overview this multi-generational approach gives me is invaluable. I know it, and my clients always point it out. They trust me with their kids because their parents trusted me as kids.

So I hope aspiring therapists, experienced clinicians, and others who are just intrigued by the subject matter find this book helpful. I offer three pieces of humble advice: figure out your specialties and never stop studying. I read clinical material (almost) daily as well as take DVD- related courses. I am always struck by what I don't know. I owe this to my clients, but I also need updated info and research for my prevention program. Kids and adults are always firing questions at me, so I need to know what I'm talking about. And holistic means just that: meds, substance abuse, diet, exercise, sleep hygiene, relaxation techniques, psychiatric disorders, medical complications, STIs, sexual development, the human body, female systems, the brain, schools of counseling… you get the picture.

Secondly, try to look at your clients from a systemic point of view. This is not easy due to family homeostasis, the scapegoating process, the focus on individual pathology, managed care, and counter-transference. We live in multiple systems that constantly interact. It never ceases to amaze me how much this is overlooked.

And lastly, never lose your sense of humor. Clinically, it balances the intensity of difficult work. Our clients usually love it, and humor makes them feel more normal. I think there is something dialectic going on here. Free expression of humor allows them to be sad and address painful issues. And it keeps us sane!

CHAPTER ONE

Approximately three decades ago, in a psychiatric unit far, far away, I was assigned a depressed sixteen-year-old with a cutting history. I saw her in individual counseling and family therapy. This was my third job in the field, with about two years previous experience in another psych unit and a local jail. I had a BA in psychology and several related grad courses. The unit I currently worked in was mixed: adults, teens, elderly, addicted, depressed, suicidal, psychotic, etc. This was the early eighties, the time of deinstitutionalization. Chronic clients, many who had been hospitalized their entire adult lives, where transitioned to less-restricted hospital placements. The goal was to get them out into the community (halfway house) and more independent. A noble but dumb idea.

So I was also assigned a fifty-year-old schizophrenic male who couldn't tolerate any of the lesser structure of the milieu. Couldn't participate in 1:1 or any group activities. Couldn't go to the cafeteria for chow. Nothing with the exceptions of smoking butts and drinking coffee. So after about a week, he freaks out and gets pink papered back to the state hospital where he's spent the previous twenty years of his life. As he's being placed in the ambulance, he sits up on the stretcher and looks at me and his psychiatrist. "I'm gonna come back and kill you both!" My first professional death threat! I figure that since he's being sent back to the state facility, I'll never see him again.

Meanwhile, I begin family therapy with my sixteen-year-old client, her mother, her older sister, and the latter's leather-clad fiancé. The mother is intense, probably a type-A personality. After one emotional session, her future son-in-law pulls me aside and says, "Have you noticed that your patient's mother is nuts?"

I'm like, "Well… ah… um… she is upset about her daughter's situation." He corrects me, insisting that she's nuts, and adds that she has a contract out on him. I'm thinking, *Holy shit is this what family therapy is like? They never told me about this stuff in undergraduate school.* They also never told me about psychotic death threats. So I figured this was the stuff you learned in graduate school.

I asked the future (or not) son-in-law what he's doing about the situation. He reaches into his vest and pulls out a loaded .357 magnum. I say, "Holy shit," and he says, "Yup, when they come for me, I'm going down in a hail of bullets."

I emphasize that one should not bring a loaded gun into family therapy. He is truly afraid, feels that his life is in danger and that he needs to protect himself. He has a permit to carry, but obviously, that's not the point. So we reach a compromise. Prior to each session, I will contact hospital security, who will lock the .357 up and then return it afterwards. When I tell my supervisor, she turns white and then agrees with the plan.

Fast forward two weeks. I arrive for my three-to-eleven shift and notice most of the patients and staff at the windows of the second-story psych unit. A staff member says, "Hey, remember the guy who threatened to kill you? Well, he's driving a truck around the parking lot, pulling a dog on a leash." I look out the window and am horrified to see this dog gamely keeping up. My counter-transference kicks in, and I'm furious. But I calm down and remind myself that this guy is very sick. The best thing to do is go talk to him.

As I approach the doors to the psych unit, they swing open, and in walks the future brother-in-law to my sixteen-year-old client, with his hand in his vest, ready to draw his gun. He announces, "Don't worry, I'll shoot him for you." The situation has gone from the absurd to the wild west in seconds.

I say, "He's sick; you can't shoot him!" He agrees with me. Meanwhile, two security guards are calming the guy down. He's pink papered back to the state hospital and the dog is okay. I continue family sessions with the weapon safely locked away. Welcome to inpatient psychiatry.

Approximately eight years after my near shootout in inpatient psychiatry, I was now armed with a master's degree in counseling, so watch out! My soft-spoken supervisor says she has a case for me that I would be perfect for. A twelve-year-old boy living with maternal grandparents who hated DSS and therapists in general. Oh, and the former social worker allegedly questioned the grandfather's intelligence during their last meeting. The latter allegedly picked up the former by the neck, so that his feet we're dangling off the ground. Now they really hated therapists! And I'm one of only two male counselors in the outreach program. I fit the bill probably because I'm the only one crazy enough to find this a challenge.

So I call the family, and the grandmother reaffirms that they are done with counselors, social workers, etc. I insist that I only wanted to be helpful and would never be disrespectful. The family huddles up and decides that they will give me one hour to make my point. I arrive at their house where I'm greeted by both grandparents, biological mom, and my future twelve-year-old client. We all sit down at the kitchen table. Tense! Tense! Grandfather gets up, leaves the room, and shortly returns with a hunting rifle (large caliber, with a scope). Silence around the kitchen table as he proceeds to place it directly in front of me. Thinking back, at no time did I really feel in danger. This was a test to see if I had any balls. So I pick up the rifle and aim it out the window.

Pandemonium breaks out! I am immediately reprimanded for being so careless around guns. I ask if the rifle is loaded, and the patriarch informs me that "you never keep a loaded gun in the house. Especially with children around."

So I ask, "Where are the bullets?"

And he says, "Locked up in a separate location. What are you, stupid?" I say that I'm not stupid, just not overly informed about guns. This is partly true, but I really like where this is headed. So he sits down next to me and for the next half hour instructs me on gun safety. He's very serious, and everybody else just nods their heads in agreement. I give them a brief description of my background and point to the clock on the wall. My hour is up. I thank them for the audition, shake everyone's hands, and leave. They're slightly shocked that it's so abrupt.

It takes a half an hour to drive back to my office. By the time I get there, the grandmother has called my supervisor. Says that the family thinks I'm great and are willing to proceed with family therapy, individual with her grandson, whatever. So, what really happened here? Counseling isn't brain surgery! This was an angry, blue-collar family that felt disrespected by social services and previous counselors. The key for me was that I never felt actually threatened. They needed respect and to feel in control. Hence, the hour audition that I agreed too. And empowerment, which they gained with my gun-safety lesson. This was one of those families that I wonder how things would have gone in a traditional office setting. No control, strange turf, a genuine fear that they could lose their child. Their fear and resistance would have provoked serious transference with a new clinician.

I worked with this family using various modalities for almost four years. They resisted systemic and individual change, disagreed with my assessments, blew me off, and blamed "the system" for many of their problems. They were always respectful, committed themselves to any treatment I suggested, and gave me an emotional goodbye dinner when we terminated. I realized that with this population especially, I needed to establish trust, empower and not intimidate, while balancing the presenting problem with the underlying systemic issues (first- and second-order change.)

> *"Jeet Kune Do favors formlessness so that it can assume all forms, and since Jeet Kune Do has no style, it can fit in with all styles. As a result, Jeet Kune Do utilizes all ways and is bound by none and likewise, uses any techniques or means which serve its end."*

> *"When there is a freedom from mechanical conditioning, there is a simplicity. Life is a relationship to the whole."*

—both quotes from the *TAO of Jeet Kune Do* by Bruce Lee

So why begin a book about a home-based psychotherapy and group dynamics with quotes from Bruce Lee? Bruce got it right! Counseling has to be fluid and flexible to meet the needs of our clients. The second line from the second quote speaks directly to the counseling relationship. Whatever the school of thought, format, or modality used, it really is all about the relationship.

This book is based on thirty-six (and counting) years of inpatient, outpatient, residential, and home-based individual, family, couples, and group counseling experiences. The last twenty years have been home-based combinations, HIV counseling, anger management with teens, adult women and men, prevention groups for adults and kids, trainings for professionals, and interventions. This book contains multiple vignettes, some not for the faint of heart. I've used these vignettes in workshops as well as 1:1 with couples, families, and in group settings. The feedback is almost always the same. People relate to shared experiences, and concrete examples reinforce the point. My approach to counseling has always been experiential and process driven. Years ago, I studied Gesalt theory, and the figure/background concept made a lot of sense to me. From inpatient clients to multi-problem families to anger management clients with axis I, axis II, axis III, and on and on diagnoses, prioritizing has always made sense. When you go to see a depressed twelve-year-old boy with a nonverbal learning disorder and his dog has just died, it tends to change the focus of the session.

Along with seeing my clients in their homes, I've also mixed modalities based on what the priority was. (That figure/background thing again.) For example, I was hired to work with a twelve-year-old girl whose parents were separated and fighting. I ended up doing individual work as well as family therapy in both of her households. This provided great continuity as well as allowing me to see her in two family settings. I could address underlying systemic factors in both settings. I truly believe that this is how kids and teens get better. So much of what is going on is age appropriate, developmental, and systemically reinforced. I can't imagine working with kids and not including a family piece. They may have substance issues, affective symptoms, PTSD, etc. But these symptoms are exacerbated by systemic factors, which are exacerbated by the individual symptoms. For example…

I was asked to run a boy's group for boys between the ages of seven and nine. Very hyper group! Billy was referred because he was angry and depressed. This group could be wild, with the kids sometimes literally climbing the walls! It was also my first experience with indirect counter-transference. Other therapists were so pissed at me because my little boy's group could be so loud. The other therapists wouldn't look me in the eye. "You need to control those boys!" they kept saying. I was really trying!

Anyway, one day during snack time, I asked each boy to say something made him really mad. Billy immediately said, "My father drinks too much beer!" As part of my treatment plan, I consulted with all the parents in their homes. This was to give them a progress report on their son's group progress (first order) and assess any systemic issues. Billy's parents admitted that his dad might drink too much, but his mother felt strongly that he was not an alcoholic because he was not physically abusive. Her father was abusive to her mother, so he was an alcoholic! Besides, Billy's father's drinking was under control. They had an agreement. No drinking Monday through Friday. On Friday and Saturday nights, Billy's mom would take his dad to "the club" where he was allowed forty beers per night. Sunday was spent basically incapacitated in bed. Monday was recovery day. Tuesday through Friday was helping with the four kids. Billy Sr. was disabled with a distended stomach, liver damage, and chronic pain. He was also on various psych meds with a diagnosis of schizophrenia. I never saw any thought disorder. He described his symptoms as having begun after witnessing horrific bloodshed in Vietnam. I think he had PTSD and acute alcohol dependency, with the latter directly related to self-medicating from the former.

So, what we had was a co-dependent and minimally functioning alcoholic family system with Billy the identified patient, diagnosed with ADHD and medicated with stimulants. I began seeing Billy and the couple/family in alternating sessions. He finished group, and I continued with him (1:1) on a monthly basis. The focus became his dad's alcohol use and his mother's expectations/enabling. Over a few months, I reframed his ADHD symptoms and depressed affect as anxiety related due to his family issues. As the focus shifted to his dad's ETOH problems and his parents' relationship, Billy became calmer and clearly more animated. His meds were cut back as his dad began to address his alcoholism.

I realized that this work probably would never have occurred if I hadn't seen his parents (initially) in a consulting role. I question whether their approach and motivation would have been different if I had consulted with them in an office. I formed a relationship with both of Billy's parents and all of his siblings. This never interfered with my relationship with Billy. This case emphatically showed me that seeing clients in their homes allowed me a chance to address second-order issues directly. I also realized that 99 percent of my clients felt more comfortable doing the work in their own home. Especially the kids! Children and adolescents give me a tour of the house, show me their favorite toys and games, as well as introduce me to all their pets. (The pets, especially the dogs, get a chapter of their own.) Outreach counseling gives people a sense of control and normalcy. In the thirty years that I've been seeing clients in their homes, I can think of six who couldn't handle it. One was an adolescent who was paranoid.

Now it is one of the primary selling points for new referrals. Most people already know that it's home based and are intrigued at the prospect. Parents inevitably say, "This must give you a better idea of the issues." Bingo. That's the green light for systems work. I immediately say that I combine modalities: 1:1, couples, sibs, family. It's up to the parents and me to suggest what course to take. My ultimate goal, which I reiterate during the initial phone consult, is to make an appointment and have the adults (or kids) tell me when I arrive who I will be working with.

Outreach also allows me the chance to use creative joining techniques that could never be used in an office. Such was the case with Erica, one of my favorite short-term (two months) adolescent girls. Very resistant! Erica was a fifteen-year-old referred by her very concerned mother. Had heard that I worked well with pissed-off adolescent girls. Mom was alarmed by her falling grades, angry affect, and oppositional behavior. Her parents were separated and awaiting divorce. Erica lived with her mom but would flee to her dad's house when things blew up. Typical scenario.

So I call her up and introduce myself. She informs me that she hates therapists and hangs up. I waited about a week and tried again. She basically tells me to screw off and BANG, hangs up again. This was awesome because I love challenges, and the feminist in me loves empowering girls. So I wait another week and call her up again. This time, instead of hanging up right away, she says, "Are you a stalking therapist?" I say no. Just that her mother is really worried and I know that I can't make the situation any worse. Then I think of the gun family that gave me a one-hour audition and ask about also giving me one hour. This appointment would relieve her mother's worry. She says, "I'll give you one hour and then leave me alone!"

I arrive at her dad's house expecting to meet Godzilla. On the way I had decided to meet with her at her house and not go for a ride (which adolescents usually ask for). I don't know her at all, except that she hates therapists, and I don't know if she has a trauma history, is paranoid, abuses substances, etc. And basically,

I don't trust her because I don't know her. I take chances, but I'm also very cautious. So I'm somewhat surprised when the door opens and I'm greeted by a beaming fifteen-year-old, all dressed up like she's going on a date. I almost say that I was there to see her sister.

I decide to be totally honest and say we don't know each other, so we should meet here. We could also walk because it's a beautiful spring day. She chooses the walking option, and away we go.

I'm glad I had my track shoes on because we walked for one and a half hours, fast, twice around her town. Some type of counseling/walking record for me. And she never stopped talking! With a record number of F-bombs like I'd never heard. Nouns, verbs, adjectives with a butt hanging out of her mouth. All I said was "How's it going?" and off she went. She begins with a vivid description of how she is firmly stuck in the middle of her parents' volatile separation. Pulled back and forth. AND SHE'S SENT TO COUNSELING! By the way, I'm leaving out the multiple F-bombs for the sake of continuity or civility or something.

So I ask her if this is why she hates counseling. She describes having been sent to a female therapist in a flowery dress in a flowery office. She is seated on a flowery sofa and the therapist places a pillow on either side of her. She says, "This pillow is your mother... This pillow is your father... You're in the middle. How does that make you feel?" (I'm cringing as she's telling me this because I know how teens HATE any patronizing words.)

Erica says, "Lady, how the fuck do you think I feel? Fuck you! I'm outta here!" (I had to include the F-bombs because it was just so Erika.) She storms out of the flower child's office. I asked her how long the experience was, and she knew, because she had been staring at the clock. Eight minutes was her counseling experience. It never ceases to amaze me how often my clients describe their previous counseling experiences as really bad. It took Erica eight minutes to learn to hate therapists!

At one point during our marathon trek, we happen by an ocean pier and she turns to me and says, "So did my mother say I'm suicidal?" I say no but add that I always do a self-harming assessment. She says, sarcastically, "Oh yeah... I'm suicidal...here I go off the pier!" She walks to the end of the pier, assumes a sprinter's starting position (in the dress, with the butt hanging out of her mouth), says again "Here I go!"

I've known this girl for one hour and think she's AWESOME. Bright, articulate, ball busting, animated, introspective, but DEFINITELY NOT SUICIDAL. Probably as suicidal as I am! And playful. The latter is huge when working with resistant adolescents (or most everybody). She looks up at me with exaggerated concern and asks: "You would save me, right?"

Now the fun begins. I say with a straight face (difficult to do). "No way... It's April, and the water is too goddamn cold!"

She acts all indignant and says, sternly, "As a therapist it's your responsibility to fish me out of the water!" Now I get serious and assure her that if she tumbles into the drink, I most definitely will pull her out. And I'd be pissed off! She stands up...brushes herself off, and says, "Well, I'm not suicidal!"

I say, "I know," and off we go again.

I'm thinking: "This girl is going to excel unless her family, the mental health system, or some co-dependent boy messes with her head." We finish our walk and Erica informs me that we should have four more sessions. I say okay!

I then called her mother, who says meekly, "Did she open up at all?" I said that she did great and requested more sessions. With teens and parent(s), I try to reassure the parents while maintaining privacy with my client. Everybody usually gets this.

Our second session immediately addresses her falling grades, why she is exhausted all the time, and why she is so irritable. Erica tells me that her ex-boyfriend is an alcoholic who calls her sobbing at night threatening to drink himself to death unless they resume their relationship. This confirms my fears about a codependent boy messing with her head. He calls her multiple times per week. She also has a close friend who is a closet cutter. The only one she talks to is Erica! She cuts late at night and calls Erica for support. Several times a week. Sometimes Erica talks to both in the same evening, which obviously stresses her out and interferes with her sleep. I've decided to be totally honest with Erica. To not be harsh, but also not sugarcoat the situation. I tell her that she is in a parentified role. Probably learned it in her family. This is the beginning of codependent relationships. She's also an enabler, a bandage for her ex and friend. Neither will get better in the long run. They need professional help, not just support from a fifteen-year-old girl. She's basically doing what I do, but she isn't getting paid for it. And it's messing up her life. I also realize that scapegoated teens get a self-esteem boost operating in a caretaker role. This is a huge issue for little girls, adolescents, and adult women referred to me. This is why I've always done well with really pissed off women. Because regardless of their own mood disorder, addiction issues, or axis II symptoms, they usually have this codependent/ parentified thing going on. They don't even realize it; plus, their loud symptoms drown it out. When I describe this scenario to Erica using other examples, she nods her head.

By the way, I think that this caretaking exacerbates their own symptoms, which locks them into the identified patient role, which in turn lowers their self-esteem. It drives them to caretake because this makes them feel better about themselves. Their symptoms get worse, which keeps the cycle repeating. And the whole process is reinforced by family, multi-generational codependency, the traditional mental health field that doesn't get this at all, social services, schools, etc. No wonder these girls are so pissed! And that's not even factoring in domestic violence and sexual abuse.

This is why the women in my adult anger-management groups like the program so much. Because as soon as I hear codependency, it becomes a major topic of conversation. Most say that they have never addressed it with a professional in depth or at all. This is very frustrating because it's so obvious. It's obvious why Erika is irritated and struggling at school. She's also too tired to participate in sports, which used to be a huge outlet for her. I suggest that she tell her ex to address his drinking and that his sobriety is not up to her. I urge her to tell her friend to talk to her parents about counseling. The following week she and her friend go to a school counselor and the friend admits to the cutting. The school counselor calls her parents.

The third session included going to the store for cold drinks. On the way back to my truck, Erica asks, "Do I look like a slut?"

I say, "No...you do not look like a slut," and proceed to ask her where that came from. She says that a boy in her class can (magically) tell who is a virgin and who is not. Allegedly, this young mind reader could go around the room, point to people, and say "Yes...no...yes...no," and on and on. I reiterate that this is nuts. She informs me that she isn't ready for sex but that being a virgin isn't cool, so she needs to look like a slut. Makes sense, in a bizarre adolescent type of thinking. This leads to a discussion of peer pressure and following what's in your heart. We also discuss the infamous double standard, the Madonna/whore dichotomy. That being a virgin is wrong and that any sexual activity makes a girl a slut. What a dynamic for a fifteen-year-old to have to grow up with. A reminder that Erica was an emotional teenager with developmental issues and a lot on her plate. She did incredible work in short time. All I did was listen, offer advice, and not be scared away by her initial bluster. Once again, it ain't rocket science. I was prepared for her because I had been taking latency aged and teen client referrals for years. Many of the therapists I knew were intimidated by the bluster. Or afraid that traumatized girls would make claims of sexual misconduct. So, I've always had my radar up.

The remaining two sessions with Erica were a review of the first three and an emphasis on her strengths (athletic ability, goals, usual grades, concern for others, honesty, and sense of humor). We also discussed sleep, hygiene, regular exercise, a healthy diet. I urged her to wait until she was comfortable about sex and to be aware of peer pressure and when the time came, always use protection. Since I was involved in HIV counseling, I cautioned her about how at risk young women were.

Erica was a joy to work with. She may have accomplished more in five sessions than anyone I've worked with. The way we left it was that her parents or she could contact me for further sessions. Her parents were relieved that she was okay.

One young mother was referred to me by the department of social service. She was pregnant and addicted to drugs, and social services wanted her to give up custody of her unborn child. Just like that! So I arrive at her darkened apartment where she is dope sick in bed. She immediately tells me to leave and call her back in a few days. No problem! Later in the counseling relationship, she discloses that she had a knife under the bed and she would have stabbed me! Okay! We worked together for two and a half years in individual counseling. Karen was literally a fighter. She would go into bars and pick fights with girls. When their boyfriends jumped in, she would knock them out too.

Karen was one of the most scapegoated clients I've ever encountered. Multiple foster placements, residential, hospitalizations, meds, NA involvement,

DSS involvement. The proverbial bad seed, with her sister the golden cheerleader. Reinforced by her family, therapists, medical people. Her social worker hated her and had no objectivity. And the hardest part to deal with was that she believed it. Would get incredibly pissed off at me if I didn't feed into that load of crap. I kept saying "Family therapy, family therapy," and she would kick and scream and say no! But she'd also be describing family dysfunction and double messages around any healthy behavior she displayed.

Actually, Karen's case resulted in my almost being physically assaulted by her mother. Can't say that I wasn't warned. Karen's anger with her mother was over the top. I would pick her up and we would take a half-hour drive to the city where she grew up. Initially, she'd be calm, and then she'd escalate and escalate. Screaming and swearing and since I was brunt of her volatility. I couldn't do anything right! If I said two words, she'd blast me and tell me to shut up. If I stayed silent, she'd say that I was useless because I never spoke up. If I responded by grunting or clearing my throat, she ripped me up and down. Unbelievable transference issues! This went on for about three months. One half hour into the ride, we would hit a rotary and head back to her apartment. Karen would escalate as we approached the rotary (near her parents' house), then slowly calm as we headed back. By the time we got back, she would be spent and silent. She'd shake my hand, thank me, and say gently with a guilty smile, "See you next week."

I had to decompress before my next appointment because my head would be ringing. I never took it personally, and when I say it lasted three months, that's how long it took. The air was out of the balloon. Karen never vented to such a level over the next two years of treatment. So it was time to gently push for family therapy. With me, because she didn't trust anyone else. Karen says no way, because her mother will freak! Will assume that I'm blaming her for all the shit that Karen has gotten into. Karen needs an ally because it really is her against the world. And the systemic brainwashing is beginning to piss me off.

By seeing Karen in strictly individual counseling, I am also reinforcing her as the problem and only one who requires treatment. This has always been a dilemma of my work. How to build second-order change into a system (individual symptoms, managed care, linear thinking) that promotes the very symptoms that I have been hired to address. And remember that the individual and family homeostasis is maintained by the symptom carrier not getting well.

So, one day Karen's mother calls me and asks to meet and discuss her daughter's progress. Gunfight at the OK corral. We meet at the local DSS office, and Karen is the most nervous that I've ever seen her. She takes me aside and says, "Remember, no mention of family therapy!" Now I'm really nervous! Four of us are sitting at a large wooden table. I'm on one side, with Karen and her parents directly across. Tense!

Karen's mother looks me in the eyes and says, "What needs to happen to keep up the progress?"

Karen whispers, "Don't do it." So here it is: THE MOMENT OF TRUTH, that goddamn dilemma! Should I rock the family homeostasis or add myself to the line of clinicians who have reinforced all the bullshit.

So I say, "I would suggest family therapy!"

The shit hits the fan! Karen gasps! Her father shrinks down into his chair; her mom bolts to her feet and reaches across the table and tries to grab me by the throat. No issues in this family! I slide back in my chair while Karen blocks her mother. Her mother storms out, followed by her dad. Karen looks at me and says, "What the fuck did you just do?" I just said that I was doing my job and was tired of her being scapegoated.

Countertransference is always alive and well in counseling. I firmly believe that the two most primary concerns for clinicians are countertransference and boundaries. Providing outreach exacerbates both. An office provides clearer boundaries for both clinician and client. The countertransference is more intense because you are right in the midst of all the systemic issues. It's tricky and can be intimidating. It's why more therapists do not provide outreach services. I used to provide outreach counseling workshops. I've come to accept that traditional therapists would rather refer their clients to me for home-based services. Usually, family therapy or adolescent 1:1. They are intrigued by the outreach model, like the idea of a minor being seen within the family system, but they want no part of the outreach experience.

I used to struggle with countertransference, especially with scapegoated kids. The systemic stuff was obvious to me and I was appalled by how scapegoated kids (and adults) could be. At least the adults could defend themselves. Schools and social services play into this. The parent or teacher or social worker refer the acting-out child for 1:1 counseling. They get diagnosed, medicated, and the dysfunctional family system maintains equilibrium. When is the last time a ten-year-old kid requested services or out of home placement or rehab for his alcoholic parents?

I believe in protecting children, but I've always felt uneasy with mandated protective reports (51-As). Or child-in-need-of-services petitions. On the surface they sound great. But in my experience, the systemic issues are not usually addressed. So, the system remains basically unchanged. And this is reinforced by the diagnostic manuals and insurance companies who reimburse for primarily medical conditions and individual treatment. It's a perpetuating cycle that keeps everything locked into first-order change. And when you see clients in their home, this dynamic is right in your face! I've seen this for thirty-five years!

At the beginning of my outreach career, I had a fifteen-year-old girl referred for individual counseling. Same MO as Erica. Depressed, defiant, staying away from home, school grades plummeting. Parents are concerned about drugs or ETOH. I begin by alternating individual sessions and family work. What became immediately obvious was that this was an alcoholic family system. They offered me alcohol during the sessions. I reiterated that they couldn't drink during family meetings and urged them to be sober for the meetings. I also realized that they had more of a comfort level because we were meeting in their home. Makes sense, I guess. Anyway, fifteen-year-old Jeannette was the only sober member of her immediate family. She was serious about school, had a boyfriend, but was clearly unhappy at home. Her parents, very concerned about her "problems," wanted her hospitalized or placed in residential. Jeannette also had a job. With me, she was punctual, verbal, never missed an appointment. And it seemed that the better she did (which I pointed out), the more they insisted on her being placed. Maybe she was schizophrenic! The family denied any substance issues and stayed focused on her.

We had several weeks between family meetings, and when I arrived, I was told by her mother that my client had been pulled out of school and sent to live with her uncle on an army base. Her mother insisted that Jeannette's behavior had been intolerable and I hadn't hospitalized her! So they did what they had to do. Remember, I was new to home-based vices and was learning on the run about systemic denial and intense countertransference. So I looked at the mother and said, "You are incredibly full of shit!" Not good at all!

Dad sinks down into his chair. Mom begins to sob. Older son (with a buzz on) arrives home and asks why mom is crying in the corner. Under a tissue, she whispers, "The therapist said that I'm full of shit." The son's reaction is, naturally, to be protective of his mother. I'm thinking that he wants to fight! Instead, they just fired my inappropriate ass! About a week later, Jeanette calls and says she's miserable. Seems that her uncle drinks nonstop when he's off duty. They allow her to return home and find a new therapist for her. Strictly 1:1, no family therapy thank you very much!

Right after the meeting, I drag my humiliated self back to the office and face my supervisor. I spill the beans. She was always supportive and said, "It sounds like Mr. Counter-Transference was in the room." I'm not very religious, but God bless her! Now I get it; I was flabbergasted that a family system could operate with so much denial, but the homeostasis needs to be preserved. And it's much worse in an addicted family system.

Transference is a psychoanalytic term that refers to unresolved, usually interpersonal issues that the intimate therapeutic alliance brings up. Counter-transference is how the clinician reacts to the transference process. I explain both processes to individual clients and group participants. Sometimes this explanation itself is a powerful intervention. People realize that they are not pissed at me, per se, but at another older male.

When I previously stated that, for me, boundaries and counter-transference are two of the most crucial factors in the counseling relationship, home-based psychotherapy magnifies the both processes. Boundaries are immediately blurred, and it is up to the clinician to sort things out. And the intimacy of being privy to personal home life exacerbates the transference/counter-transference issues. One last clinical vignette illustrates how complicated things can get.

About the same time as my countertransference, I was referred a depressed twelve-year-old girl. Long-term social service involvement, with suspected sexual abuse. Two sisters and one brother in a single-parenthood, female-headed family. Dad minimally involved in the family. This girl was brilliant and stunningly beautiful. When she had makeup on, she could pass for seventeen. She was significantly depressed, so I began seeing Natalie weekly in individual counseling. I registered one of her younger sisters so I could work with the family. This was how I proceeded with multi-problem families. Individual counseling with the identified patient to address individual symptoms, work on their self-esteem, and reinforce healthy behaviors. Family therapy to reframe my individual client's issues and identify and address underlying systemic issues. First-order and second-order change at the same time. Just made common sense! For Natalie, this meant encouraging school effort, avoiding drugs and alcohol, and accepting the fact that she was twelve (too young for dating and sex even though her older peer group was into dating and sex). She also was becoming more and more parentified due to her mother having mental health issues and a brother who was acting out. Actually, the latter was the original referral for counseling, but he resisted the process. Naturally, much of Natalie's self-esteem was tied to her parentification and looking much older.

So this case had many of the repetitive features of other family and individual referrals. During a consult with Mom, the bombshell was dropped. It seems that during Mom's individual counseling at a nearby clinic, Natalie and her sibs would sit in the waiting room. Both she and her brother had this gut feeling that something wasn't right. Apparently, Mom's individual sessions included sex. Natalie said that she knew that "something wasn't right." Her mother had a lawsuit against this therapist and the agency he represented.

My involvement with Natalie and her family now took on a whole new facet. The individual sessions proceeded as usual. The family sessions proceeded as usual. But I had to reassure her mother that I WAS NOT SEXUALLY ABUSING HER DAUGHTER while providing a sympathetic sounding board for her mother as she proceeded with the lawsuit. Not taught in undergraduate or graduate school! My anxiety and counter-transference were kept in check by my grounded and calm supervisor. But I couldn't discuss the case with other therapists because their anxiety would shoot sky high, which would trigger mine. I should stop seeing the family! I should transfer Natalie to a female therapist. I was going to be accused of something because I was male, Mom's transference issues with male therapists, her potential for disassociation, and on and on.

Meanwhile, I'm working with a precocious, parentified girl who is being hit on and pressured by her sexually active friends. And I'm reading the court depositions and reassuring her mom that I'm not being inappropriate with her daughter. While reframing Natalie's individual symptoms and addressing systemic and parenting issues in the family meetings. I worked with this family for three and a half years. Natalie held off on being sexually active until she was sixteen and a half. Insisted that she would have to care for the person and that the setting had to be romantic. No backseat romance! I continually reassured Mom that Natalie was being safe, cautious, and thoughtful. I could only imagine her mother's fear and anxiety. Plus, her court date was approaching. Fortunately, she settled literally minutes before the proceedings were about to begin. She moved her family to another state and bought a house. They surprised me months later by stopping by my office to say hello. That was very emotional!

I think Natalie's case was the most intense and significant work that I've ever done. EVERYBODY (except for my supervisor) was telling me to bail. The transference and counter-transference were through the roof. The systemic work went on: I confronted Mom's parenting, reframed Natalie's age-appropriate behavior, pissed everyone off, was temporarily fired, and then rehired. I stood on the sideline and supported her mother. And I was careful (really careful) with my boundaries. As a result, we had mutual trust. I think the family learned that they could navigate through some serious bullshit with a supportive and appropriate male therapist.

This is why I question the effectiveness of brief counseling with multi-problem cases involving trauma. Think about all the reasons Natalie, her mother, and family had not to trust me.

Home-Based Intervention

When you really think about it, all outreach or home-based services are a type of intervention. Whether it's a parent calling for family therapy, a spouse inquiring about seeing the couple, a depressed and angry son, an alcoholic sister, some type of behavior is being targeted. So, when people call and ask if I do interventions, I think *my whole life is an intervention.* Sometimes, it's the real deal like you see on reality television. So, this is how I proceed.

I meet with the initial contact person and concerned family and friends to introduce myself, discuss the problem, and decide how to proceed. I averaged one to two traditional interventions per year. I'd say 50 percent are successful. I like to get as many people involved as possible. Parents, children, sibs, close friends… Anyone who has a legitimate and loving concern for the identified person. After all the potential participants are identified, they are invited to a preliminary meeting. I reintroduce myself and ask for each person's thoughts and concerns. This is when I find out about the consensus and who thinks what about the situation.

Part of family systems work is addressing first- versus second-order change. What has been called "change of change." This means us unbalancing the family system or upsetting the equilibrium. From a systems point of view, the addict or alcoholic or individual with untreated mental health issues has a role in keeping the system, although dysfunctional, operating.

This is the part of the reason addiction work is so challenging. You are not only treating obsessive and addictive practices, but you are unbalancing homeostasis. Once again, this may be dysfunctional, but it preserves equilibrium. Change, positive change is anxiety provoking because it is different. This is why I've always been sensitive to children, teens, and adults. Because they usually have a negative role in the dysfunction.

This is part of my mind set during an intervention. What do I mean by being successful? Engaging in further treatment, entering a rehab or hospital, scheduling a detox—and following through, scheduling a medication referral, agreeing to see another therapist. That's the plan for the identical patient. For the family system, success is committing to treatment and coming to a consensus about the (1) need for immediate action and (2) the specifics of the issues involved.

This is when things can get murky? Does he really have an addiction issue, or does he just like to party? He might be an alcoholic, but does he use drugs? He might have a problem with prescribed opiates. You know, for his back pain. But he would never ever use heroin! He ran out of his prescribed Percocet and bought some Oxycontin on the street. That doesn't make him an addict, right? So why are we here?

Substance use and abuse, especially alcohol, may be long term and chronic. The family may know about enabling, on an intellectual level. But they need to be involved, which can be threatening. Will they have to look at their own use? It's classic systemic denial, worsened when other family members drink or smoke. And exacerbated even more when they drink or smoke with the object of the intervention. Because then they feel guilty and begin to question their own substance use.

If the person is a functioning addict or alcoholic, the denial is worse. He works hard, pays his bills, loves his family. And they clearly do not want to believe that he's behind on bills and spends ninety dollars a day on opiates.

One concerned husband complained of his wife being alcoholic, in denial, and refusing to acknowledge any addiction issues. I met with him, her parents, and his two adult children. Everyone said Sheila drank throughout the day. Morning till night. Probably enough to prevent withdrawals. She drove intoxicated and drank heavily on her free time. She was also an executive, the primary breadwinner. Never missed work and very responsible.

Sheila blasted her husband, tried to throw me out, accused her father and mother of betrayal, and minimized her son and daughter's concerns. What changed her mind was a consensus ultimatum. If she didn't enter treatment that day, husband, son, and daughter were moving in with her parents. Everyone was crying! The deciding factor was when she saw their bags packed and ready to go. She had a bed waiting at the nearby rehab. She completed the rehab and, I hope, did follow-up treatments.

If the family system exhibits addictive patterns, it gets even murkier. The intervention may have been requested due to a family member using a new drug of choice (weed instead of alcohol). The family as a whole may be in total denial about their substance usage, with no intention to stop even if this reinforces the identified client's behavior. One such family was shocked that after whatever treatment took place (detox, rehab, AA), they should consider alcohol-free parties or not inviting their nephew if alcohol was being served. Was I nuts? No alcohol at a party? This is the classic double message that I see all the time! Don't drink or smoke while we surround you with chronic substance use and abuse.

I ask everyone to write down their concerns, because in the heat of the moment, people are crying and angry and caught up in the addict/alcoholic's denial and defensiveness. Usually, something has worsened for the individual or system for someone to reach out for help. In my experience, the major complications include the client being an adult and not deemed committable. Not psychotic, not imminently at risk to themself or others. Legally old enough to decide whether they need treatment or not. They could be broke, chronically unemployed, depressed... basically dysfunctional. It's still up to them!

Enabling has usually gone on for years, at an individual and family level. Loved ones have "been thinking about an intervention for a year...I've had your number," which has made the process more ingrained. Everyone has their roles in the situation. Dad is pissed and insists that "you're out in one week" (never happens); Mom enables, as does Dad but in a more subtle manner; sister studying to be a social worker who specializes in addictions is rallying the troops to do something about her brother. She enables too. He has dropped out of college (again), hasn't found work, and lives at home. Doesn't pay room and board because he has no money (except for weed). Smokes and drinks. Mom knows that something is wrong, because at ten years old he was diagnosed as ADHD. She's very protective!

One family had been ripped off by their opiate-and-benzodiazepine-addicted son for years. They had to lock up their wallets in a safe every night and secured other valuables in a locked room. Their son refused rehab, engaged in NA meeting, worked part time, and lived at home. Participated sporadically in family therapy, went back and forth with whether or not he was using. The family was stuck, with both parents at odds about what and what not to do. Dad was the heavy, while Mom feared for her son's life. We never really had a formal intervention. I find that these families get motivated, lose steam, and go in and out of treatment. My first goal is to assess safety concerns. Then I try to get the couple to agree on how to proceed. Sometimes when I use the "intervention" word, it scares them off. I think this is because they still have a level of denial.

Interventions are messy and anxiety provoking. I EXPERIENCE MORE ANXIETY! As mentioned before, the situation is exacerbated by an absence of reciprocal trust between myself and the identified client. Every intervention is different. The first question I'm asked is "should the person be told? Or should it be a surprise/ambush?" It's a catch twenty-two: if you tell them ahead of time, they may not show up. If you surprise them, they often do feel ambushed. In one large intervention (twelve family members), the consensus after much debate: don't tell him. Just about everyone said that Mike would definitely not show up if he knew what was going on. So the night of the intervention arrives. UNBELIEVABLE tension! I'm usually relaxed, but I walked in and hit a wall of anxiety, accompanied by tears and intense stares. Mike walks in and looks stunned at the gathering of people he hasn't seen together for years. I stand up and introduce myself. Shake his hand and explain what's going on. He says "fuck this" and leaves. End of intervention. Actually, his brother followed him out and they went for coffee. I encouraged the relatives to be vigilant about their concerns, keep talking to Mike about the severity of the situation, as well as reminding them to not enable. Not fall into previous patterns. Basically show him that something has changed. This was obviously not a successful intervention.

Mike's case was a great example of how far apart everyone was on the extent of his addiction. One uncle refused to consider him an addict. (He'd never use drugs.) Somebody else feared that he would commit suicide in front of his kids. His wife, looking profoundly depressed, just cried. Some urged her to take the kids and not return home. I think they needed ongoing family work and individual counseling following the intervention.

Another intervention involved a dysfunctional eighteen-year-old male. He was told prior to my arriving and urged to attend by both his parents. He left and never came back. I still have not met him. The intervention included his mother, stepfather, sister, and biological father. The latter lived in another state. Everyone was concerned about his substance use, unemployment, apathy, and suspected affective disorder. When things heated up at his mom's house, he would bounce to his dad's house. Back and forth with no resolution of the issues. Significant second-order change occurred when Dad agreed to not let him relocate to his place. Everyone would give him the same message: you have to remain at Mom's house and address your problems. Both families would remain in contact concerning his progress. When given the plan, he chose to move out and live with a friend. Since he had no source of income, this was temporary, and he returned home. He attempted to move back to his dad's place. His dad again said no. I met with this family a total of three times and bumped into the mother one and a half years later. Her son was back home and functioning better.

So, what really happened here? A resistant adolescent, two family systems agreeing on a strategy and following through with the plan. Less enabling and more empowering. With the parents allowing the teen to exercise independence and then allowing him to return home with limits. Since I never met the object of the intervention, I guess that you could call this a systemic intervention. Whatever works!

Once again, I usually have no relationship with the individual in crisis. So my biggest challenge is establishing trust, or at least respect, on the fly. I'm viewed as an adversary, allied with the family, and confronting often serious denial. Who is this guy who thinks he's an expert? And being a systems guy, I always question deep down inside whether the family is reporting accurately. So I offer to meet individually with the identified client to hear his side of the story. Initially, they're usually too pissed to do this. But the goal is for immediate treatment. Not to be accepted and trusted for a long-term counseling experience.

A Few More Words About Enabling

The American Heritage Dictionary defines "enable" as "to supply with the means, knowledge, or opportunity to do something. To make feasible or possible. To give legal power, capacity, or sanctions. To permit." In my world, I would add personal gain (self-esteem, reassurance, lesser guilt) as motivation to enable. Or personal or financial gain. This goes directly to systemic factors such as the mother who allows her addicted daughter to use for fear of sobriety leading to independence and the loss of her daughter's social security disability (which pays her rent).

People throw out "you're an enabler" all the time. I always encourage my clients to empower, not enable, but this can be complicated. I worked with a couple who had a very disturbed son with Bipolar II symptoms and an addictive personality. Both parents enabled, but the dad accused Mom of supporting his habit, always giving in, never following through. A need for more "tough love." She would remind him of the same approach he used with their adolescent daughter. He kicked her out and she overdosed on Fentanyl and drowned. Mom would glare at her husband and say, "You're responsible for our daughter's death. I won't let that happen to our son!"

By the way, whenever the son was sober, his Bipolar II symptoms were almost absent. Periodically, and while intoxicated, he would get arrested and put in jail. An intervention via the criminal system. He was always healthy when he got out. This also took the back and forth between his parents out of their hands.

CHAPTER TWO

Foster Family Therapy

As previously mentioned, years ago I worked for a counseling agency that provided outreach services to adults, teens, children, couples, and families. My caseload included a number of DSS referred foster children. Short term, long term, preadoptive, with the reasons for removal including neglect, trauma, and physical and sexual abuse. One boy who was referred to me was sexually acting out with his foster sibs. Foster mom was understandably freaked, and I divided my time with 1:1 sessions and consults with foster mom. The situation was exacerbated by three other foster children having sexual abuse in their backgrounds. They were triggering each other and engaged in almost obsessive sexual play.

Increased individual counseling and constant observation by the foster mother was not making any clear changes, so I decided to try a different approach. I suggested to the foster mother that we begin having weekly family therapy sessions with the kids involved. Address it as a group issue since it involved all the children. The kids were nervous but admitted to the sexual behavior. I was nervous because no one else at my agency was running home-based group sessions in foster families with sexually reactive children. But all the kids had individual counseling, and I had excellent supervision. One of the first things I noticed was how important the foster mother's presence was. She presented a consistent and stabilizing maternal object. I also appreciated how difficult it was for her to hear about graphic sexual behavior in her foster home. This behavior was openly (but not punitively) discussed with expectations and boundaries. Within three weeks, the sexual acting out was diminished significantly. I continued to see my individual client on a weekly basis.

The other children continued with their individual therapists. With the initial family, I was struck by how effective this approach had been in quickly addressing a serious issue. I began to rethink my approach to working with foster kids and conceptualized a foster family therapy approach. Since my approach to pathology was family systems and interpersonal, it made sense to address these issues using a systemic modality. Several of these foster placements were chaotic with their own family and individual issues. At times I felt that biological family issues were not being addressed and that my client was being scapegoated, in part because he was a foster child with obvious behavioral, affective, and developmental issues.

I also realized that many of these foster children were repeating their specific roles and behaviors learned in their family systems. Parentification, domestic violence, codependency, victimization, secondary gains, testing of limits, and parental authority were all getting played out in these foster homes. The foster parents (especially the moms) were stressed out and probably depressed. The biological family issues (developmentally normal otherwise) were wrapped up in foster child issues.

This was uncharted territory as a counseling modality for a number of reasons. Most of the therapists (outreach) provided individual counseling to minors or adults. Other agency clinicians saw individuals, couples, and families in their office. When I asked around, seeing foster families was not utilized. Most of the clinicians were symptom (depression, ADHD) or behavioral (fighting, truancy) focused. I researched and found minimal work with foster family systems. With a systemic approach—some as biological systems—to addressing underlying issues. For me it was obvious, that Gestalt figure/background thing. How to proceed made sense. Plus I could assess the health of the foster home, offer a sympathetic ear to (oftentimes) overwhelmed foster parents, and reframe behavior.

Since I had one individual client in each foster home, I didn't want to interfere with our weekly counseling relationship. So I would register another family member (foster or biological) and bill to that client for foster family sessions. Occasionally, this became complicated due to my new client already being involved in 1:1 counseling. For the most part, this wasn't an issue because I coordinated services with the individual therapists. And they were happy to see systems work getting done, due to the extreme stress level of their clients.

For me, the best part of providing foster family therapy and individual counseling in a home-based setting was the continuity this provided for my clients. Nine-year-old Carla was removed from her home and placed after her mother relapsed on prescription drugs. Carla was placed in one of the foster homes I was working with, so she initially got to know me in a family session. She needed a 1:1, and I had an opening. I saw her weekly in foster family therapy and twice a month in individual counseling. I consulted with her foster mother and her school. The plan was for reunification, so, eventually, we had meetings at DSS with her mother. When Carla began to transition back home with overnight visits, we moved the family meetings from DSS to her mother's apartment. So I consulted with her mother. Throughout this process, I continued seeing Carla individually. When she returned home, we alternated individual and family sessions. We were also able to do termination work with her foster family.

When I think back to Carla's case, I get incredibly frustrated. I'm no genius, but isn't it obvious that the process of Carla's treatment facilitated great continuity? And isn't it obvious that the multiple settings gave me a view of her demeanor and mood, along with other significant people in her life? I'll say it again: this ain't brain surgery. Most of it is common sense. My frustration comes from seeing this format in action and realizing that I was the only one doing it. A combination of unorthodox clinical interventions. Outreach, mixing modalities, foster family therapy! I worked with five foster family systems for a total of approximately five years. I was left with these impressions:

#1 The concept of opening cans of worms replaces the traditional can of worms. Some of these families had five foster kids along with biological sons, daughters, nephews, and nieces. Every foster child arrives with their own individual and family baggage. Otherwise, they wouldn't be foster kids. The foster families themselves had varying degrees of affective symptoms, addiction, and personality disorders. One of the most popular foster mothers I worked with was probably borderline. Sometimes I felt like I was fishing in an overstocked pond!

#2 These family systems were primarily matriarchal: all but one had two parents. Dad had a full-time job out of the house. Mom's full-time job was foster parent. Mom usually co-led the family sessions. I always invited the dads, but work schedules made their regular participation difficult. The transference issues between the foster parents (especially Mom) and the children were immediate and extreme. Part of my role was explaining this to the adults. Many of the kids came from single-parented (matriarchal) systems with abandonment and trauma issues. And either no father figure or an abusive father figure. Foster mom was clearly the lightning rod. I saw her role as paradoxical, swinging back and forth between the idealized/ rescuing maternal figure and abandoning figure.

#3 These sessions combined group dynamics with family systems theory. A heterogeneous group who live like a family but are usually not blood related. As with group and family systems, I saw scapegoating, parentification, and idealization. Acting out foster kids were perfect scapegoats. Projective identification was always a huge factor, because, once again, this involved multiple kids, systems, and trauma experiences.One way I addressed the scapegoating was to branch off and have biological family meetings. This took some of the onus off the foster kids and provided second-order family work. This is a great example of the "butterfly effect" from chaos theory, which we will discuss in another chapter. Simply put, being referred a nine-year-old foster female led to consults with the foster mother, which led to foster family therapy, which led to biological family therapy, which led to 1:1 with the foster mother. Intense 1:1 around her family background, affective issues, parenting issues, and self-esteem. And, by the way, this individual worked lead to foster mom deciding to cut back on her foster care referrals and focus on her biological family.

#4 The issues discussed in these sessions included neglect, physical and sexual abuse. They were often horrendous, and I remember one foster mother who needed support after particularly difficult meetings. In one family session, I had four latency-aged boys disclose incest in their family. I had three foster siblings disclose significant physical abuse in their previous foster homes.

You could tell immediately who was parentified by the way they took control and acted the big sister or brother role. The acting-out children and adolescents received negative attention, which facilitated the projection identification (the kid who lies, becomes the liar, who gets secondary gains, attention from that liar role). Trauma victims inadvertently repeat behavior that invites negative attention. So they remain some sort of victim.

A corollary of this was the burnout rate and visible exhaustion and depression I saw with the foster parents. Several were adult children from alcoholic family systems, and I believe that their natural inclination was to continue caretaking. So they needed support around boundaries, realistic expectations, dealing with referring agencies, and differentiating between pathology and developmental behavior. The latter might include an incest survivor showing age-appropriate sexual curiosity. Some foster parents would overcompensate due to the extreme deprivation that their kids had endured. The children couldn't appreciate the excess, and the foster mother was left feeling burned out and unappreciated. I'm reminded of one foster mother who tried to provide as lavish a Christmas atmosphere as possible. One room was literally two feet deep in presents. Her foster kids became overly competitive, basically ignoring any presents that were not expensive or up to par with other gifts. Foster mom became tearful and furious.

#5 A general feeling of lack of support or information from referring protective agencies. I worked with these families during an era of budget cuts and dwindling resources. As I mentioned before, many of these placements were of an emergency nature with minimal information provided. I would arrive for a weekly family therapy meeting and be introduced to a new foster child. One referral had a history of violent outbursts, but nobody told the foster parents. That particular situation was further complicated by the fact that, historically, this female had pattern of attacking biological (specifically female) children. She was referred to a household with a fourteen-year-old daughter, whom she subsequently attacked. In some cases, victims of alleged sexual abuse were placed with other reactive children, such as in the case which started me seeing foster families.

I heard complaints of spotty referring info from every foster system I worked with. As a result, I made several suggestions. First! Ask the referral source specifically about any reported history of sexual abuse, perpetration of sexual abuse, fighting, running, drug or ETOH abuse. Also ask for the number of previous placements and some bio family background. I also suggested that they ask whether the placement was to be short or long term, pre-adoptive, or was there a plan for reunification. Also, were visits back home part of the plan? Because this was a delicate issue. I saw foster kids triggered with heightened anxiety and exacerbated behavioral issues before and after the onset of renewed contact. Makes sense! But this was usually interpreted as a regression due to being reintroduced to an unsafe environment. Maybe...maybe not. A further complication for the child and families involved was the fact that the referring agency was legally obligated to schedule home visits, even if the long-term plan included the loss of parental rights and subsequent adoption. Confusing, isn't it? It certainly was for my clients. Secondly, I suggested writing out a contract that the referring agency, foster parent, and child signed in regard to expectations and family rules. Because they were minors, I don't think that this would have been legal, but I still think it made sense.

#6 Longer term foster family participants developed a process that could be very creative. One family, on its own initiative, created three subgroups. The first half hour included the whole family (minus the dad, who was working). The second half hour was devoted to "big kid's time," including foster mom and three fifteen-year-olds (two female, one male). The three younger children (ages six, seven, and ten) were allowed to leave the meeting, so that the adolescents could discuss dating, sexuality, and birth control. Age-appropriate stuff. This taught boundaries and provided a safe forum for discussing sensitive material. An additional half hour was included to address issues of a more confidential nature with myself and the foster parent(s). This particular family system came up with the entire format. I just sat, nodding my head while thinking *this is awesome*!

#7 These sessions provided important information for individual therapists, biological parents, and social workers, lawyers, and physicians. I was repeatedly amazed at the wealth of disclosures and personal information that came out of these meetings. I think it would be fair to say that a level of trust and comfort developed in the foster family group process. Winnicott's holding environment, or more specifically, a safe family environment with a grounding maternal figure. With loyalty clearly remaining for the biological family. An aspect of this that I never saw coming was the general enthusiasm of the kids and foster parents involved. Very different from the grunts and groans and rolled eyes I'd get from kids in biological family sessions. I actually had kids who cancelled outside activities so as to not miss the meetings. I was asked if we could lengthen the meetings or meet more frequently. I was confronted if I was late. Or if I missed the point. Or if I was too pushy...or not pushy enough, and they came up with many of the rules. For a therapist who empowers and encourages healthy decisions, it didn't get any better. I can only go back to the nurturing environment that allowed these usually traumatized children to speak up, problem solve, be assertive, be funny and spontaneous.

Working with five foster family systems was a small sample. But the most recurring issues addressed included:

#1 Sexual abuse victimization and/or perpetration of sexual abuse. This was present in four of the five cases, with three of the referrals made due to sexual acting out with foster sibs and neighbors. As mentioned before, the foster parents were given little or no information concerning sexual abuse histories or potential acting out.

#2 Systemic issues regarding the nuclear family were being displaced by more urgent foster child issues. I realized that in some cases, the foster child issues were a detouring mechanism. The biological family issues were masked by the foster kids "with problems."

#3 Abandonment issues with maternal figures due to having been removed from primarily single-parent families. I've already mentioned the tremendous transference issues with the foster mother, which could trigger her own issues. These kids blamed the social service system, protected their families, and denied the extent of the abuse or neglect. What else could they do? Or what else could they know, based on long-term, normalized abuse and neglect. Plus, many had attachment issues, so establishing trust and intimacy was a process.

#4 Foster children reprising their family roles as scapegoated, parentified, defiant, bullying, and victimized. In foster care, the projective identification gets played out, and the family of origin drama repeats itself. Looking back, I think that this was the most crucial issue to be addressed. Addressing and confronting this behavior in a safe and more neutral environment with an objective, professional person available. This was where the group dynamics and family systems work became intertwined.

Back to my frustrations providing foster family therapy. I've already mentioned that I was engaged in a tremendously exciting format which nobody else that I knew of was doing. So I did a training at my agency and quickly realized that other home-based counselors either didn't have family systems' background or were 1:1 oriented. Then it got worse. I was asked to provide a workshop for a foster service agency. I was really excited because I could describe this work to social workers and foster parents. They hated it! I was stunned until I began looking at it from a family systems' point of view. Describing foster family pathology and process was too threatening. The elephant in the room. Or second-order change. Shaking up foster family homeostasis.

This was incredibly frustrating to me because the feedback I was getting from foster parents, kids, the social workers directly involved with those kids, and biological parents as well was all positive. Two foster parents told me that it was the most effective form of counseling they had ever seen. Based on mood and behavioral changes. The social workers urged me to contact the educational divisions of their agencies. They went to their supervisors, who also advocated for training either in the central or local offices. No responses! I reminded myself again that this was extreme family systems' work, second-order change, and very threatening to the traditional school of thought. Everybody wanted higher functioning foster homes, better trained and supported foster parents. To provide safe environments for victims of abuse and neglect. As I mentioned before, it's often done on an emergency basis. The kids are the identified clients, like in a biological home where the adults request services and the children are the identified patients. First-order change reinforced by the medical model, school system, and social service providers. And therapists who provide an individual orientation and background and proceed with involving only the referred child.

Foster family sessions stopped after approximately five years when I went into private practice and decided to not use medical insurance. These families couldn't afford private pay. They were not happy about discontinuing the meetings, but I had made my decision. Looking back, I could have continued doing agency work and focused on foster family systems' work. But I would have missed out on other clinical experiences, which have been great. Plus, I was tired of advocating for a service that the clinical world apparently wasn't ready for.

I decided to finish this chapter with my process notes from the first four sessions involving a foster family made up of two foster parents, two biological daughters, five foster children, and multiple pets. One biological daughter attended the meetings intermittently. Regular participants included:

Joan and Bruce (parents)
Anne (bio daughter, age 19)
Foster sibs: Jackie, age 16
Ruth, age 14 1/2
Carl, age 15
Jack, age 10
Teddy, age 8

Jack and Teddy were brothers. I had been Jack's individual therapist for three years. Working with Jack meant that I knew everyone in the foster home. I knew Teddy from my relationship with his brother and had seen both in their biological family. I consulted with Joan and Bruce and offered advice concerning all the kids. Teddy had recently discontinued seeing his therapist, and Joan was concerned about his lack of work around alleged physical and sexual abuse. She inquired about my seeing Teddy in 1:1, but we both wondered if this would interfere with my relationship with Jack.

So I told Bruce and Joan about my experiences with foster family therapy. Teddy could still have his own individual therapist, and we all knew and trusted each other. We agreed to proceed with the meetings, but only if Jack was okay with it. He was! Both parents were also considering adopting both Teddy and Jack. They felt that the family sessions could provide a smoother transition. Made sense to me!

Session one: Participants included Joan, Jackie, Teddy, and Carl. Bruce, Jack, and Ruth were unavailable for the meeting. This was an informational meeting to present the plan to the kids and field any questions. Joan, Teddy, and Jackie were enthusiastic; Carl was quiet. Prior to these meetings, I had had the least amount of contact with Carl. I explained what foster family therapy was all about. We immediately discussed rules, particularly confidentiality. What was said in the group would remain in the home, although I would be allowed to share pertinent info with individual therapists and social workers. We would take turns providing snacks. One person was to speak at a time. No violence would be allowed. Participants were free to say what they wanted, but house rules concerning language were to be respected. My hope was that, eventually, everyone would reinforce these rules.

Jackie presented as the most verbal, and immediately sounded parentified. Talked about her strained relationship with her dad, which Joan reinforced. I told her that she sounded parentified and wondered if her dad was alcoholic. She confirmed that. Both boys were quiet but attentive. Carl had learning issues, which put him at an immediate disadvantage in a verbal household. We discussed a regular time to meet that would not conflict with outside activities.

Jackie's disclosures about her family alcoholism allowed me to introduce and explain alcoholism, codependency, adult child issues, and the scapegoating process. The first session was clearly a "joining" and informational family therapy meeting. Toward the end, I asked those attending to speculate on how Bruce, Ruth, and Jack would have participated. The clear consensus was that Dad would have acted like a therapist, Jack would have never stopped talking, and Ruth would have just sat and cried.

Session two: Participants included Joan, Jackie, Jack, Ruth, Teddy, Carl, and Anne (biological daughter). Everyone except for Bruce, who had work commitments. As I mentioned before, this was not unusual for most of the foster family sessions. Anne sounded just like her mother, very verbal and assertive. She was also direct and nurturing. A great role model for Ruth and Jackie, and a nurturing, strong female figure for the boys. I had pointed this out several times while inviting her participation. She had resisted ("I don't do therapists"), but she was present!

The meeting began with Joan apologizing for Bruce not being available. Assured me that he would be at the next meeting. Anne was in and out, waiting for a ride. I suggested that her coming and going meant that she really wanted to attend. Everyone was enthusiastic. Since several family members were not available for the initial meeting, we reviewed the rules. I then asked everyone's age and where they were in school. I also asked for the circumstances that brought each one into foster care. I asked what their legal status was (pre-adoptive, plan to return home, guardianship). Also whether or not they were having scheduled visits with their biological family.

Both Jack and Teddy started to get antsy. Jack (remember that he's been in 1:1 with me for years) said, "Let's go… Let's do what we're here for!" Jack knew me the best and was taking the lead. How could I not love that? Since I'm always process oriented, I commented again on and coming and going, Anne was told that this represented her role in the family (in and out). So I asked what her impact (leaving) had on the family. Both Jackie and Ruth immediately said they had added responsibility with Jack and Teddy. They disagreed on how to "parent" their younger foster brothers. Ruth was the stricter of the two, while Jackie was looser but harsher. Joan was slightly speechless and stunned that both girls saw themselves as caretakers.

At one point, Jackie was sitting on Teddy, tickling him. Anne had Jack in her lap and was lightly smacking him in a good-natured way. Both boys were absolutely loving it. They were clearly the favorites in their foster home. They'd been there for two years and their bio mom has abdicated parental rights. The family was very protective due to their reported victimization histories. I remember thinking *this is exactly what these boys need*. Strong support and tactile affection to hopefully compensate for what they didn't get in their biological family. I pointed out how significant this was in the meeting.

What this affection triggered in both Teddy and Jack were disclosures of abuse from their mother's previous boyfriend. This was especially significant for Teddy, who said little to his 1:1 therapist. Jack had openly discussed it with me. I realized that this was a combination of feeling safe in a family atmosphere (while literally being held) and role modeling by the older brother (to discuss sensitive family secrets). This was a common dynamic in all my foster family therapy sessions. They took turns telling anecdotes, culminating with severe beatings that led to a trip to the hospital. The hospital filed 51-AS, and both boys were removed. The other participants were stunned by the graphic disclosures. For Teddy, it was like a dam breaking, the way the information poured out of him.

The second meeting left me with several impressions. Teddy was now ready to disclose. Jack was struggling with having to share my attention with the whole family. Jackie's control issues surfaced around increased stress. Both she and Ruth acted parentified. Carl was clearly the scapegoat. People talked over him and through him. They complained that he was sneaky (passive aggressive), which was probably the only means of drawing attention to himself. No one was tactile with Carl. This was probably partly due to his being an adolescent boy. Parentified roles had shifted since Anne moved out. And this was clearly a matriarchal family system.

Session three: Attended by Joan, Bruce, Jackie, Ruth, Carl, Jack, and Teddy. Meeting began with my being confronted about being late. I had a habit of being late and they reminded me in a good-natured way. I knew that they trusted me enough to confront me. Very cool! I also realized that I was more confrontative of them. (Trust works both ways!) I also thought they had the ego strength to be confronted more directly. I processed the second meeting (partly due to Bruce not being available for either of the first two meetings). I felt confident that they wouldn't be scared off from what I said and they had the insight to understand it. Goes back to mutual trust.

Carl began talking and was immediately talked over by Jackie, Teddy, and Jack. I pointed out that this has occurred in all three meetings and that it was rude. I said that nobody listened to what Carl said and it must hurt his feelings. Carl was embarrassed by the attention. I asked the family why nobody seemed to care what Carl said. The family reiterated that they disliked his sneakiness and his tendency to be physically inappropriate. Joan immediately defended Carl by saying that he was doing better with being physically inappropriate. Carl was somewhat slow, and my guess was that he wanted to act like the younger sibs and have a tactile relationship. But he was fifteen and close in age to his foster sisters. I reiterated the scapegoating process, which I observed with Carl and admitted that he needed an ally (in the family meetings). Meaning me! Jack was obviously threatened by this alliance and immediately tried to set Carl up. He rolled a ball by Carl's chair and insisted that the latter return it to him while once again interrupting Carl as he tried to speak. Carl didn't buy into it and ignored the provocation. (Maybe because having an ally empowered him.)

Carl then disclosed that he can't live with his biological sister because he had twisted her arm and broken it. I wondered, once again, if having an ally helped him disclose in the group process. His disclosure then led to Teddy and Jack disclosing further abuse. Maybe they were triggered by Carl's disclosure. Or maybe they were being competitive. (So you think what you did was bad?) Teddy then stunned the group by saying that he was given the choice of having his fingers or penis cut off for having gotten out of bed and looking out the window. Thankfully, Mom's ex didn't follow through!

After being shocked into silence, the family erupted in a protective manner. Consensus was that they wished this guy was still alive so that they could "kick his ass!" Jack said that he wished he knew where this guy was buried "so that I could piss on his grave." Holy shit! Talk about countertransference! It was times like that when I realized how important clinical experience was. I was both appalled and outraged by what I heard and fueled by the group's outrage. By the way, everyone supported Jack's right to urinate on his grave.

The subject matter then turned to why their mother hadn't protected them. I cautiously reframed her behavior as someone acting out of fear due to her history of being victimized. I also referred to my own countertransference giving me mixed feelings about their mother. At times, I pitied her, and at other times, I was really angry.

With these disclosures, the floodgates had been opened. Jackie began talking about her alcoholic father and how she felt excluded by her dad's new girlfriend. Talked about her parentified status, and I reframed this as normal adult child (of alcoholic) behavior. Ruth disclosed her mother's deteriorating mental health due to her history of bipolar disorder. Said that her mom had long periods of serious depression. (Which explained to me why she could act so parentified at times.) I explained how children of parents with physical or psychological (or both) problems are still adult children with control issues, low tolerance to stress, anxiety, and depression. Ruth added that her parentified position increased as her mother got sicker.

37

Remember when I was told that Ruth would just sit and cry? She was actually verbal and very insightful, for fourteen and a half. I had also been told that Bruce (foster dad) would act like a therapist. He basically took a background role for his first family session. He had to be stunned by what he heard, as far as the graphic nature of the disclosures. He also didn't have the benefit of the first two sessions (rules, introductions, and background info). Both Jack and Teddy told anecdotes involving their foster father. The themes were of support, approval for showing initiative, with an obvious lack of any intimidation. A safe adult male! The meeting ended with my congratulating everyone for their honesty and openness with me.

Session four: Participants included Jackie, Carl, and Ruth. The schedule was disrupted due to a holiday and my not getting a call from Joan to cancel the session. Since I was also scheduled to go on vacation for two weeks, all three wanted to meet. The major topic was school, and the major theme was Carl still trying to not be talked over by his two foster sisters. All three enjoyed school, which was refreshing for me. Their school attendance was consistent, and because of that, they were allowed one "mental health day" per semester. Jackie described this as "when you wake up and feel like shit and don't want to do anything." Regular school attendance was an expectation in this family. So the "mental health day" rule was a reward, and the rule was not abused. Another sign of a healthy family system!

This was a light meeting with funny stories and good-natured barbs thrown at me because I was going on vacation. They also were curious as to why I chose to be a therapist. Jackie said that she was interested in pursuing a mental health career but admitted to being intimated by years of school. I've always been enthusiastic about my work, and all three commented on this enthusiasm. Since we were in the initial stages of treatment and I would be away for two weeks, the focus of the session was reinforcing age-appropriate behavior (and feeding their self-esteem).

Four foster family therapy sessions with a new (for me) system, but individuals who I had a varying degree of relationship with. Two joining meetings, one intense session, and one light, ego-supportive session. One month! This was typical of my work with foster families. Systemic family therapy with traumatized children in a safe and nurturing environment. When I could emphasize their strengths and development issues, I could also further empower both foster parents. This positive regard freed up discussions of past abuse and individual concerns. I was privileged to be part of this.

CHAPTER THREE

(a) HIV and AIDS Counseling

(b) AIDS Awareness Prevention Groups

In 1992 I was referred a family of four (mom, two sons, one daughter) with the major precipitant being Mom having an AIDS diagnosis. This was around the time the meds improved dramatically and people could live for twenty years with HIV infection. Prior to the introduction of the "Cocktail," life expectancy could be as short as a few years. It was bleak, to say the least. And the AZT always made my clients sick. In the beginning of the pandemic, the choices were horrible: either be chronically sick and live a little longer or discontinue the meds and die of AIDS-related complications. These included cancer and pneumonia.

I knew very little about HIV and AIDS, so I began to consult with an AIDS case management organization. When they learned that I specialized in substance abuse and provided group psychotherapy, they asked me to facilitate dual-diagnosis groups at their agency. Clients with addiction issues and HIV infection. So I did! Shortly after, I was contacted by another HIV/AIDS organization that, using Ryan White funding, provided counseling sessions to people with the virus. They were especially interested in my outreach approach. They had contacts with numerous therapists, but most saw their clients in traditional office settings. Plus I did family work with multi-problem systems. Several years later, I accepted a part-time position as the clinical director of the same organization that had hired me to run the dual-diagnosis groups. When I left that position, I was offered the chance to run a prevention program, or what I called "AIDS Awareness," for various adolescent programs and schools. A great example of the butterfly effect, which will have its own chapter. If you had told me that one outreach family would lead to HIV specified cases, HIV support groups, clinical specialist for an AIDS organization, and offering prevention services to approximately twenty overall sites including high schools, alternative high schools, middle schools, alternative middle schools, group homes, DYS facilities, a YMCA, a YWCA, a women's prerelease program, several shelters, several parenting programs, and DUI groups, well... AIDS awareness will be discussed in chapter five.

So now I was an HIV specialist! Some people thought that I only worked with an AIDS population. While writing this chapter, I realized that this entire book could be about my approximately twenty-five years of HIV-related counseling. So, where to begin? With my clients and families that suffered from this truly bizarre and complicated disease.

First of all, I thought I'd be dealing with bedridden, dying people in their grieving families. Instead, I was working with a familiar population: multi-problem families and clients in their homes. Addiction, affective disorders, personality disorders, poverty, eating disorders, unemployment, homelessness, and schizophrenia! Along with HIV infection and hepatitis C infection (maybe 30 percent of the time). As treatment got better, the focus shifted. From death with dignity (providing basic needs and support) to managing a chronic disease (working, dating, holistic health techniques). As with all my work, a huge emphasis on substance abuse.

In the early days of AIDS, working with dying people made me a better person. Made me appreciate my health. Made me appreciate the strength and compassion of people dealing with a terminal illness, potent meds, side effects from the meds, side effects from the second set of meds that helped you deal with side effects from the first set of meds. James was one of my first HIV+ clients (with an AIDS diagnosis). In recovery from benzo addiction, depressed, and labeled as schizophrenic. I think that was an incorrect diagnosis. His wife was paranoid and would have psychotic episodes and call the police. James was also a heavy smoker and would be periodically hospitalized for lung congestion. He may have been the kindest person I ever met. Never said a hostile word about anyone. When I think of role models in my life, I think of three: my older brother, Martin Luther King, and James.

I also had my own denial thrown in my face. I watched Magic Johnson's press conference, where he disclosed his HIV+ status. (He was an amazing basketball player who tested HIV+ in 1991.) He was strongly urged by his doctors to retire. He also unequivocally maintained that he had never shot drugs or had sex with a male. Right around the same time, I was referred a young married guy who had been tested and also found to be HIV+. And he swore that he had never touched IV drugs or had sex with a male. And here I am, running support groups in counseling men and women with the virus. And although I was sexually selective (bullshit) and limited my partners (more bullshit), I didn't always use a condom. I rationalized that I was a heterosexual male who didn't use drugs. These two cases slapped me right upside the head, and I immediately scheduled a test.

This was when it took two weeks to get a test results. I was fine on the way to the clinic to be tested. But on the way back to the clinic two weeks later, I was scared shitless. Thinking about anyone I've been with for the past ten years. As I tell my clients now, one new partner a year is a lot of indirect sexual exposure over ten years. I remember sitting in the waiting room, "casually" reading a magazine. Only problem was that I was shaking so much, I couldn't concentrate. What made matters worse was that I had a cold (or flu), so I had several of the acute symptoms of HIV infection. Low-grade fever, upper respiratory congestion, and, yes, night sweats. I think the latter was imaginary or hysterical. But, whatever, I thought I was fucked!

I was so visibly freaked that the nurse ran over and said, "Your test was negative," and I bet I've told that story in one hundred prevention groups. I told it in an adolescent female substance program. When I left, they all marched into the director's office and demanded to be tested. They were, all with negative results.

What a truly bizarre virus this is. Sometimes my counseling sessions went like this: ten minutes talking about HIV status and fifty minutes discussing all the side effects of the meds. Sometimes serious side effects, like diabetes. One women's support group spent entire sessions discussing lipodystrophy. This phenomenon produces metabolic changes, fat loss, and fat accumulation. It's thought to be medication and virus related. People suffering from lipodystrophy can have enlarged stomachs (also called "crix belly" due to the relationship with crixivan, which was a popular protease inhibitor.) They could also develop a hard lump on the back of their neck. This was called the "buffalo hump." And the "triple chin," which was what it sounded like. At the same time, they could have fat losses in their arms, legs, and face. The latter would leave them with a drawn, sunken look.

So most of my women's HIV support group was spent discussing these physical changes, self-esteem (or lack of), and managing other med side effects. They were young, so they wanted to date and have relationships. Can you imagine having all this on your plate? I also remember the "drug holiday" fiasco of the mid-nineties. At that point, I didn't have any HIV+ clients, but I had my prevention program in full swing. I was also fortunate enough to have a speaker's bureau, four women and three men with the virus. Two of my female speakers contacted me about a temporary discontinuation of their meds. They had made tremendous gains over the previous year. Their viral loads were undetectable and their CD-4 counts were rising. The theory was that a cessation of the cocktail might jump start a healthier immune system. After one month, the results were disastrous. Plunging CD-4 counts and exploding viral infection. That was sad, because people thought that the meds might not have to be daily and lifelong.

HIV meds were always complicated. Bruce would greet me at the door, pale and having raccoon eyes. Constant nausea and explosive diarrhea. Having to consume food (while nauseous) to help metabolize the meds. Sometimes he'd eat, throw up, and then eat as quickly as he could. Or he would greet me at the door with bright eyes and color in his cheeks and a bounce to his step, had just worked out at the gym, cardio and weight training. This meant he had stopped his meds, so the virus was multiplying like crazy. His infectious disease doctor would read him the riot act. For the whole time we worked together, Bruce went back and forth. He wouldn't have it any other way. Who could blame him?

Thomas was my client and then my speaker. HIV+ for twenty years; full blown AIDS for nine years. He was wiped out and emaciated, bedridden a lot of the time. Serious lipodystrophy symptoms. I went to see him one day, and Thomas informed me that he was done with the cocktail. This was in the fall and he believed he would die before Christmas if he continued with the meds. He had informed his doctor, who tried to talk him out of it. Thomas's rationale was that he had lived with HIV for twenty years. He was done fighting and wanted to let God handle the rest. I was ambivalent but felt strongly that this was his choice to make. Two weeks later, I went back to see him. He wasn't bedridden anymore! He was gardening and informed me that his appetite was back and that he had gained ten pounds. He was healthy for about six weeks and then developed an opportunistic infection, pneumonia. He was hospitalized, lost the weight he had gained, and returned home. Put on weight and resumed landscaping. Developed pneumonia again and was hospitalized. Got better and went home again. Throughout this back and forth, he refused to resume taking the meds. My lasting memory of Thomas was when he emotionally and emphatically spoke to one of my alternative high school groups. They were acting all ADD, and he blasted them for their inattention around a life-or-death situation. He really looked bad, and I suggested that he should be home in bed. Nope, he insisted on "talking to these kids so they might never have to go through this." Two weeks later, he developed pneumonia again and was hospitalized for the last time. He died in respite care with family around him, calm and at peace. I wonder, if he had stayed on the (improving) meds, would he be alive today? Maybe, but maybe not.

I was referred a fifteen-year-old girl whose mother had an AIDS diagnosis and was deteriorating quickly. So our work could have been described as pre-grief counseling. She was obviously angry that her mother was sick. She was also furious that her mother had put herself in a position to be infected. So our sessions were a mixture of anger, sadness, and depression. Cathy talked about what she would say at her mom's funeral. The impact on her brother and father. And the fact that along with her sadness, she was really pissed off at her mother. And was it okay to be angry with your dying mother?

So, once again, the bizarro world of HIV kicks in, and the meds dramatically improved. Her mom's health took a 180-degree turn and she's out of bed and much healthier. Now, Cathy was unsettled due to cognitive dissonance. Months of preparing for the inevitable and saying goodbye. Finding a balance for her confused emotions. After all, she was only fifteen! So now she was relieved and pissed and guilty about being pissed. Strange dynamics, to say the least. Her case brought up a systemic issue. Her brother was an active addict who was enabled by her family. When the mom got better, my focus shifted to the effect that his addiction had on my client. She was parentified, worried, and questioning whether she should go away to college (and not look after her brother). I remember my conscious treatment shift and her father not being happy about it.

But that was HIV counseling from a systemic point of view. It was never, and I mean never, just about the virus.

Cathy had an unbelievable sense of humor, and this was woven throughout our sessions. I was scheduled to see her, and her mother called and informed me that Cathy was hospitalized on an emergency basis with the "flesh eating virus." What? Had it on her mouth. Seriously? So I asked her mother if I could visit her and she gave me the okay. I knocked on her door and she told me to enter. On the way to the hospital, I was trying to be upbeat and wondering how to be therapeutic. I mean, really...a fifteen-year-old girl with the flesh-eating virus (on her face, no less), her mom has AIDS, and her brother is an addict.

So she sat up in bed and with exaggerated affect says, "My mother's got AIDS and I've got the flesh-eating virus on my face...I'm totally fucked!" I cautiously hugged her and morphed into Robin Williams as best I could. We made fun of hospital food, diseases in general, and told jokes. For the whole hour! In the two years that we worked together, Cathy reminded me that what we did that day was exactly what she needed. Remember my quotes from Bruce Lee? Sometimes you need Freud; sometimes Robin Williams. By the way, Cathy was cured of her herpes-related condition and went home.

Home-based psychotherapy with HIV+ clients and their families could enter the surrealistic realm when you least expected it. Nancy was referred to me for individual counseling and family therapy. Family included a sixteen-year-old daughter, Donna, who was freaked about her mother's condition. So I alternated 1:1s with Nancy and family sessions with her and Donna. This eventually led to individual counseling with Donna. Nancy's medical condition was extremely serious. A healthy person's CD-4 count might be one thousand. An infected person goes from an HIV+ diagnosis to an AIDS diagnosis when their CD-4 count reaches two hundred or below. Nancy's CD-4 count was nine. This meant that she had some opportunistic infection going on at all times.

When the counseling referral was made, nobody mentioned that addiction was a major factor. In fact, almost everyone in the immediate and extended family was addicted to opiates, painkillers, and prescription and nonprescription drugs. So the counseling included HIV, managing vegetative depressive symptoms, and chronic systemic substance abuse. Opiates were the primary concern of the family.

Like many of my clients, they felt that if you were clean from dope, then benzodiazepines, weed, and ETOH were not that big a deal. To complicate the situation further, Nancy was prescribed multiple meds for her medical conditions.

This family had serious drug issues and would periodically run their own internal interventions. Someone would be particularly out of control, and that person would be strongly urged to enter detox. Strongly, like that episode in *The Sopranos* when they staged the intervention for Tony's nephew, Christopher. By the way, when I watched that episode, I said, "That's what my clients do!" So these interventions could end with bruises, hard feelings, and someone in detox. I guess you could call that very tough love.

One day I was scheduled to see Donna, and she was running late. I sat in the living room, chit-chatting with Nancy. She was visibly nervous, which was totally out of character. So I asked her what was going on, and she informed me that the family had conducted an intervention the night before. With her son who had been strongly urged to enter detox. He was scheduled to go the next day but was currently dope sick. He was allowed to get high one last time and was currently in the bathroom, shooting up.

Mom admitted to being nervous because I was her counselor and her adult son was sitting on the toilet with a needle in his arm. Good point! I'm thinking, *Am I liable if he overdoses and falls off the toilet?* And, *Am I enabling an addictive family by sitting and twiddling my thumbs?* and, *She's my client and strict HIV/AIDS confidentiality applies,* and *He's an adult and not a minor.* And *Isn't this supposed to be about AIDS?* But I reminded myself that I had signed on for all of this: seeing active addicts in their homes, many with AIDS. I also reminded myself that they had a plan, a fucked-up plan but still a plan. So suck it up and do your job!

Nancy looked at me and said, "I am very uncomfortable sitting here."

I said, "Me too!"

She yelled toward the bathroom, "Christopher, don't come out; my counselor's here."

He yells back, "Okay, Ma." At least he wasn't dead.

I reminded Nancy that my appointment was supposed to be with Donna. She suggested that we wait outside. She could wash her boat. I asked what I could do. Apparently, Donna had a vegetable garden, and Nancy asked if I wanted to water her vegetables. I was just relieved to be out of that house at that point. I grabbed the hose and began doing something that they never talked about in graduate school. So now the situation goes from weird to really weird.

I'm sweeping the hose over healthy tomatoes, green peppers, and beans and, bang, a healthy marijuana plant! Three feet high, with buds. So I made the decision not to give a contradictory message and went around the poor wilted potted plant. Everything else got drenched. Donna arrived home and immediately confronted me about not watering her weed.

HIV counseling solidified my decision to incorporate addiction/substance abuse counseling into every population I worked with. Anger management, family therapy, adolescents, holistic groups, prevention groups, and workshops for teachers, clinicians, and childcare workers. Timmy was another HIV+ client (actually, he had an AIDS diagnosis) who reinforced this. Timmy was a chronic substance abuser who was on methadone maintenance for his heroin addiction. He also smoked cigarettes and marijuana. A lot of marijuana! He had the wasting syndrome and insisted that smoking weed stimulated his appetite. The problem was that THC was a banned substance, and he was told that if his drug tests continued to come back dirty, he would be kicked out of the methadone clinic. He insisted that if kicked out, he would immediately start doing dope since he was dying of AIDS anyway. Two interesting things happened. He stopped smoking and was bedridden for several days. Looked dope sick. The first client I ever had the crashed so bad from discontinuing marijuana use. He couldn't get off the sofa and just waved me away, saying, "Come back next week." I thought he might be dying. So when I showed up for our next meeting, I was shocked when Timmy greeted me at the door, actually chipper, and said, "Let's walk for our session." We never walked for our sessions. This was the result of laying off the weed for one week?

He had also been prescribed Marinol for his appetite problem. This was allowed by his methadone clinic even though it was basically a pill form of marijuana. This was before medical marijuana was legal, and the thinking was #1, Marinol is a legal drug and could be prescribed, and #2, his tests should show the same level (if he took it as prescribed.) Smoking different amounts of weed would alter his THC levels. There was one problem. The Marinol, which was concentrated THC, was so powerful that it made him trip. Said he took it as prescribed and tripped for hours. And this, from a person who had been smoking weed since age twelve and using heroin since age eighteen. So we took out one of his Marinol and split in half. This was the dosage Timmy ended up using to combat the wasting syndrome.

Timmy's case brought up the number of mixed feelings. On the one hand, he couldn't take a hit of THC because marijuana was illegal. But he could take a concentrated THC pill that made him trip like he was doing a hallucinogenic. That was okay because it was prescribed. And I'd bet, deep down inside, his physician would have preferred the marijuana. But he couldn't prescribe a federally illegal drug. On the other hand, I was amazed at the transformation I witnessed when Timmy stopped using marijuana. He was a different client. I'd use his experience with other clients around pros and cons of smoking marijuana.

People have asked me for thirty years about my countertransference with HIV/AIDS clients. Of course, they don't call it that. They just ask, "Are you scared, worried about your health?" That's an easy one to answer: No! It also offers a teaching moment. As long as I'm not having sex or coming in contact with blood, the risk for me is zero. I thought I'd be more uncomfortable. I wasn't, but my buttons have been pushed around several AIDS specific themes.

I've been triggered the most by HIV+ individuals (predominately men) who knowingly have put HIV-people (mainly women) at risk for infection. Some of it is denial; some is male narcissism. Sometimes it's due to fear of test results, so the individual refuses to get tested but keeps practicing unsafe sex. Sometimes it sounds like sociopathy, like "If I get infected, I'll just infect as many women as possible before I die." Sometimes it's selfishness, like "I don't like how condoms feel...but I don't want to infect anyone." There is also a creepy vindictiveness (once again, usually males) concerning a sexual partner (usually women) putting them at risk. "I'd kill the bitch!" I think that attitude also reflects a lack of up-to-date info. They still think HIV infection means AIDS, which means a death sentence. So it's a knee-jerk reaction to someone trying to kill you.

Years ago, I was referred an HIV+ woman who was infected by her husband. He had full blown AIDS, and she was cognitively limited and suspected nothing. Six months later, I was referred another young woman who was infected by the same guy. Weird situation, counseling two women infected by the same guy. One of my speakers in AIDS awareness was infected by a guy who had already infected three other women. They had been practicing safe sex for several months. At that point he promised her he had been tested and was negative. He lied and knew he had full blown AIDS. It gets worse! She participated in a support group for HIV+ women who were all infected by fiancés, boyfriends, and husbands. And *most* knew that they were infected. Another one of my speakers was infected by a guy who turned it around and accused her of infecting him.

I worked with two couples who were serially discordant. The guys were HIV+; the women were HIV-. So, of course they practiced safe sex 100 percent of the time, right? Wrong! The first couple used condoms 80 percent of the time, so they could enjoy sex more part of the time. The second couple! Well, here we go back into the bizarro world of HIV counseling. They immediately had unprotected oral, vaginal, and anal sex; her rationale was that she loved him and didn't want to live without him. His rationale was that she was willing to have unsafe sex. By the way, they had been dating for about two months. Oh, and she had a young daughter. So I pleaded with them to use condoms and urged her to get tested when the window period had passed. Their relationship lasted for another month and she went online and announced to the world that this selfish man had put her at risk for AIDS. The reaction was amazing! Half the people who responded jumped all over him for his selfishness. The other half (mostly women) criticized her for going public with his medical condition. The poor guy. Several felt so bad, they reached out to him and offered to date him. I'll never forget what he said to me. He was truly bewildered by the response and said, "I never had so many interested women...until I got AIDS."

So if you are unfamiliar with the AIDS phenomenon, you are probably unaware that criminal liability and penalties vary from state to state. In my state, putting someone at risk for HIV or actually infecting them sexually carries no penalty. Of all the things I've said in my prevention groups, this is the showstopper. It's that cognitive dissonance thing happening again. Can't be true! In some Southern states, it's criminal to have sex at all, even safe sex, if you are HIV+. You're considered a sex offender. But in Massachusetts, the expectation is that we will keep ourselves safe by practicing responsible behavior. Can't argue with the responsible behavior part. This thinking was, in part, based on the history of discrimination towards HIV+ people. Remember Ryan White? The young hemophiliac who was denied school admission, then went to court for his educational rights? Then he was further harassed and ended up switching schools? The other rationale for not holding someone potentially criminally responsible was that people would be more open about their positive status, would get tested more regularly, and would be more consistent with medical treatment. It all makes sense. But as a therapist, I look at the factors that get in the way of keeping people healthy. Selfishness, denial, narcissism, dependency issues, personality disorders, and substance abuse.

One thing that surprised me was that my clients and speakers who were put at risk and subsequently infected were in support of the Massachusetts's personal-responsibility approach to HIV prevention. Don't get me wrong. They were incredibly pissed and often fantasized about being Lorraina Bobbit. But for most of them, it went back to discrimination from doctors, dentists, family, employers. Everyone I talked to was discriminated against multiple times.

A dentist lied about his schedule being so booked that he couldn't accept new patients. Until an HIV case manager threatened to blow the whistle. An emergency room physician placed an eight-foot table between himself and one of my speakers. Wouldn't get any closer. She verbally blasted the doctor and went to another hospital. A family member served dinner on fine china and insisted that my client use paper plates. Another speaker was not allowed to swim in the family pool. These were professionals who should knew better and "loved ones" who needed to know better. Is there any question why my clients and speakers guarded their privacy?

So I wasn't surprised by the shock and initial anxiety when I casually mentioned that the next week we would have an HIV+ speaker visit our group. Adults were usually okay; but latency-aged kids and teens would often shake their heads in protest. "You can't bring someone in with AIDS… We'll breathe the same air and get sick." I'll never forget bringing Sharon to my little girls' group at a local Boys and Girls Club. They were eleven to twelve years old and informed me that they would run out of the room. I reminded them all that they were not at risk. So the next week Sharon and I were sitting at the front of a classroom when my girls walked in. Six of them! They all stopped and immediately hid behind any available furniture, poking their heads out to see the AIDS lady. Sharon was a veteran with this stuff. So she laughed and casually said, "You're in no danger because we're not having sex and I'm not bleeding." First they poked their heads out again, and then began to move closer. Then they sat in chairs, at a distance. Then they moved the chairs closer... and then a little closer. By the end of the group, they had formed a semicircle around the two of us three feet away. When Sharon got up to say goodbye, my alpha asked if she could hug her. Then they all lined up and hugged her. It brought Sharon and some of these girls to tears. For several years after, whenever I ran into any of these girls as adolescents, they would also inquire about Sharon's health.

My own countertransference was exacerbated by eclectic counseling experiences. I might be providing anger management to chauvinistic and insensitive young males while sitting with women who were HIV infected by their boyfriends. Or having two sixteen-year-old girls disclose they were violently raped and that the perps tested positive for HIV. So these girls were being treated with PEP (postexposure prophylaxis) and praying that the treatment would work. Oh, and one of these girls had hepatitis C and wondered how the cocktail would affect her liver enzymes. It was times like that when I realized the benefit of having a lot of experience in multiple issues.

I was running a men's anger management group, and one young participant was complaining about his pregnant girlfriend being a bitch. Some of this was posturing, I'm pretty sure, because young guys often would do that at the onset of anger management. ("Yeah... Look at me. I'm a badass in anger management.") So he announced that he was dumping her for another woman. He tells the group several weeks later that is new girlfriend is also a bitch and could possibly be pregnant by him, so he's dumping her too!

I always tell my clients that they can think things but not act out on the thoughts. He was sitting to my left and my immediate thought was how far I could knock him out of the chair with one punch. No countertransference going on there! I took some deep breaths, reminded myself that I was teaching anger-management techniques, and moved on to another part of the curriculum. I used cognitive and behavioral techniques. The same thing I teach my clients. During the "role models of anger," when I ask my clients to describe how anger expression was modeled for them during childhood, this same person shrugged and said he couldn't say because he was in eight foster homes. I realized that this guy goes from relationship to relationship because he has attachment issues that mirrored his childhood. I pointed out how his background contributed to his unstable relationships. I think he got it.

The other HIV-related issue for me has always been infected children. Almost always infected at birth, because Mom was asymptomatic and didn't feel the need to get tested. This was twenty years ago. Now, HIV screening is a part of pregnancy and only about 1 percent of newborn babies have the virus. When you take everything into consideration, this is probably the greatest HIV treatment progress. I was the family therapist for two HIV+ little girls. The older one wasn't diagnosed until the younger one became symptomatic. When Mom was asked if she'd ever been tested, she said no. She was asymptomatic, plus her husband was regularly tested for his work. His results had always been negative. And they both were monogamous, so why get tested when she got pregnant twice? Mom and both daughters tested HIV+. The older was still asymptomatic, but the younger (eight years old) had a CD-4 count so low she was approaching an AIDS diagnosis. Dad was tested again, and he was HIV-. Mom contacted the guy she had dated ten years earlier, and he had full blown AIDS. Since it's much more difficult for a woman to infect a man during intercourse, Dad was healthy.

This info has always been the second showstopper in AIDS awareness. That you could have been infected ten years earlier and be healthy...and highly infectious! And that an HIV+ woman might not infect her partner. It's that cognitive dissonance thing again. That happened a lot in prevention groups. What? You're saying that the law doesn't protect us? That I might not get infected if I have unsafe sex (especially if I'm a man with a female)? That I can be HIV+ and not be sick? That I could have been infected by the guy I dated nine years ago and now I'm getting sick? That HIV+ people still have sex? That they don't always tell their partner? And that's not a crime? That it isn't just a government or pharmaceutical conspiracy to prevent a cure and make more money? That it isn't a manmade virus? And there isn't a cure? What about Magic Johnson? He's cured and healthy! He's healthy but still HIV+.

Anyway, I digress. Both girls were put on the meds, and the younger one recovered fairly quickly. Their combination therapy included taking multiple pills three times a day. Both were perplexed as to why they had to take so many pills when they were not sick. Both their parents were afraid that neighbors or school peers would find out about their HIV status and their daughters would be ostracized. The family would have to move. Since this was twenty years ago, this was all possible. So the girls were told that they had a virus in their blood that they had inherited from their mother and that their blood was infectious. All accurate info without the words HIV or AIDS. The younger daughter figured it out first after reading about HIV. "Is this what we have?"

Both parents were incredibly guilty and showered their daughters with material things. The couple was obviously stressed but did the best they could. Both girls were spoiled and somewhat entitled. Their parents gave them whatever they wanted because they didn't know how much time they had. HIV was not yet considered a chronic infection because HAART (highly active anti-retroviral therapy) was in the early stages. Some of the early meds were horse pills, large capsules with the ingredients preserved with ETOH. After barely being able to swallow these beasts, my clients would be slightly drunk. Another weird HIV curve ball. When a powdered form came out, the meds could be mixed with pudding or applesauce. After the meds improved, these girls were healthy as horses. In time, with their family, they were never sick.

My role as family therapist was limited to support for the family and the couple. It was all about health, meds, privacy, guilt, and staying positive.

A fourteen-year-old male also infected at birth was warned by his extended family to avoid intimate relationships because that's how his father infected his mother. Both were deceased. He was a personable and handsome young man whom girls were naturally attracted to. So he avoided any advances, which was picked up by other kids. Soon he was teased for being gay. So he cut his hair and dressed all macho. This was at a time when my clients took meds three times a day. He had a noon dosage that he received from the school nurse. Since he was afraid that other students would notice a pattern, he varied his route to the nurse's office. We are talking about a middle school child. Talk about tearing at your heart! On a positive note, as the meds got better, so did his health. I never knew him as sick.

Thankfully, HIV is now a more manageable disease. The medication has fewer side effects and fewer dosages. Along with post-exposure prophylaxis, there is pre-exposure prophylaxis, which lowers the viral load to what's termed undetectable. At this level, it is difficult to transmit the HIV virus. A vaccine has been in the works for thirty years. The negative side to this progress is that due to a lesser HIV symptoms, many people choose to practice unsafe sex. This leaves them vulnerable to other viral and bacterial sexually transmitted diseases. The latter are more easily treated but remain serious infections.

CHAPTER FOUR

AIDS Awareness

Which brings us to my AIDS awareness prevention program. Fifteen years ago, the HIV case management organization that I had worked with in different capacities was given a five-thousand-dollar grant to provide prevention services to adolescent girls. Since I did outreach and had networking contacts and got along with resistant teens, it was a good fit. The grant specified young women due to the sharp increase in HIV infection within that population. Especially for drug users, sexual partners of IV drug users, women of color, and victims of sexual abuse. Since this was prevention, I targeted middle school and high school ages, young moms, women in pre-release programs, alternative schools, residential programs, YWCA's, and Boys and Girls Club. I began with a local high school and residential program for adolescent girls. Then I added a Boys and Girls Club as well as a STARR (short term diagnostic) program. It was mostly word of mouth. The fact that it was free was a big selling point. I targeted one specific community due to the high rates of HIV infection and intravenous drug use. In that particular city, I worked with an adolescent girl's substance abuse program, a group home for addicted women, a teen living program, a YWCA, and a day treatment facility. The latter was for clients with mental health and substance issues.

These groups morphed into additional groups with new participants due to staff requests. For example, a latency-aged girls' group was added when staff noticed adolescent boys hitting on ten- to twelve-year-olds. Since the program curriculum included sex ed and because HIV prevention involved intimacy discussions, I provided sex ed. I brought in books in Spanish and English. I catered to the age group. For example, I took an abstinence approach with the latency group and a safe sex approach with the adolescent groups. Since this was AIDS awareness, I taught the "ABC" model. Abstinence minimizes HIV infection risk. If you choose to be sexual, be monogamous. And use condoms for all types of sexual activity. I limited the info provided to the latency groups and told them that the adolescent curriculum was different. We also sent consents home so parents could sign off on their child's participation.

AIDS awareness groups were poignant, depressing, hilarious, and enlightening. After two years, I was contacted in September by a representative of the company funding the program. She wanted to sit in on a group and make sure that the five thousand dollars was being used wisely. The problem was that I had ended in June and hadn't resumed the program. Three and a half months with no contact with any of the girls. So I walked around the Boys and Girls Club and found four previous group members. I filled them in on what was happening and assigned a topic we had covered to three of the girls. I asked each to say a little about what they had learned the previous year. The topics were HIV, puberty, and avoiding child molesters. I had decided to make avoiding child molesters part of the sex ed after one twelve-year-old described an incident where she was grabbed by an adult male, thrown down, and escaped by stabbing him with a pen knife. Staff was enthusiastic about adding this piece to AIDS awareness.

I rounded up the girls and hoped that they would remember enough to validate my program. The representative arrived—very formal—and I led her into a room with one table and several chairs. We were soon joined by four loud, dancing, and singing eleven- and twelve-year-olds. One was carrying a blasting boom box. It was then that I assigned the topics. No notice!

I introduced Ms. Brown as the funder for my girls' group. "So she's the one who pays you?" somebody said. I said yes and that she was making sure that her company's money was well spent. After the introductions and assigned topics, the group dynamics began with a flourish. First these young ladies insisted on dragging the table to the middle of the room. They placed the chairs around the table and informed the adults that they would take turns standing on the table while discussing the specified topic. The first talked about HIV and AIDS. Accurate info including condom use, unprotected sex, needles, a disease of the blood, no cure. The puberty discussion was hit or miss, but parts of it were spot on. By the way, whenever someone was finished, they bowed and received loud applause.

But I knew that the avoiding sexual predator topic would be the highlight, because twelve-year-old Sophia was the group leader and a firecracker. She just loved to run the show. Up on the table she went and said, "So you're walking alone through the park and some old guy like him"—she points at me—"begins following you. Says something like, 'Hey, little girl, I've lost my dog. Can you help me find him?' You don't approach him. Just walk away. Keep a car's length between him and you. If he keeps following you, go to a nearby house and pretend that you're going home. Look for a house with kids' toys, so it makes sense. Knock on the door and scream that you're being chased. Yell really loud!"

I asked Sophia what to do if he grabs you. She looked at me and said, "Do what this guy taught us. Go for the eyes and go for the nuts! Then run away and go home. Find a couple of my Puerto Rico uncles. Then they go find the guy and kick his ass!" Sophia bowed and jumped off the table to a tremendous round of applause.

I looked over at my group funder and noticed that she was no longer as composed or relaxed. Was it my imagination or did she look slightly disheveled? Looked like she had sat through an hour of my screaming little girls' group! I asked everyone to thank her for coming. Then the boom box roared, and the dancing and singing began. The representative was in a hurry, so I walked her to her car. Was it my imagination or was she wobbling a bit? Her head was probably spinning because my head was always spinning after these groups. It was probably bombastic for someone who wasn't familiar with the process. All she said to me, very softly, was, "Are they always so loud?"

"Always," I said.

I can't overemphasize how proud I was of these girls. Yanked off the basketball court or from some other activity, with ten minutes notice. To remember and repeat to a stranger info they hadn't reviewed for months. And they had retained a lot! Especially Sophia. She knocked it out of the park! With the exception of getting Puerto Rican uncles to kick the perp's ass, she remembered everything. She acted the alpha, both blustery and booming, but she also repeated lifesaving lessons. At times like that, I realize that this specific information was the most important issue I could teach these girls. And that I was blessed to have the resources for providing free services to a vulnerable population.

So I wondered how our guest would react to her wild group experience. I always wonder how people "sitting in" will react, because I'm desensitized to the chaos and most everyone else is not. Plus, I consider the zaniness part of the process. Anyway, one week later, I was contacted by the director of the agency I represented. The grant had been doubled from five thousand to ten thousand dollars. Pretty cool, huh? I was able to increase the number of groups. Shortly after that, a second grant allowed me to target latency-aged and adolescent males.

As AIDS awareness grew, I developed questionnaires, tests, teaming activities, and evaluations. Some type of measurement of effectiveness. This proved to be impossible due to vacations, inconsistent participation, emergencies, and, in some cases, staff indifference. Or staff burn out. Or staff turnover. The last could be very frustrating. New staff might be hired and discontinue the program because they had no relationship with me. No trust! The groundwork for this trust was built on face-to-face consults. My role included filing 51-As, on rare occasions taking kids to get tested, making referrals to 1:1 and family therapists, as well as contacting parents and legal guardians.

The sex ed aspect grew out of necessity. I was shocked by what they knew or didn't know. In one group, only one of seven knew that she could get her period at any time. I referred them back to their mothers to find out when they had begun menstruation. They came back shocked! "My mother got her period at twelve...and I'm twelve...which means..." I began to include bilingual sex ed books, because half of my girls were Dominican or Puerto Rican. When I asked how much sex ed they had received, silence and blank stares. Very little in school. And the subjects of sex and pregnancy were never discussed at home. "If I bring this stuff up at home, I'll get my ass kicked!" I heard this multiple times. Talking about anything sexual meant that you were considering sex or already engaged in sex, so you took a beating. This mentality blows my mind. These days, I still sit with adolescent women in young parenting programs who confirm that taboo topic of sex when they were children. But they also have this knee-jerk reaction when I ask them at what age they'll talk to their kids about the birds and the bees. Until they really process it, they usually say, "Sixteen. They'll find out on their own like I did," and this is while sitting in a federally subsidized home for young mothers who readily admit that they wished they had waited.

At the same time, these latency-aged girls have been exposed to inappropriate or bizarre sexual material. One of the "I didn't know I could get my period" girls also asked me why people have sex with farm animals. While looking over her uncle's shoulder, he was apparently watching bestiality. Nice! I asked these girls who they could talk to about puberty and sexual development. Parents? Oh no! Siblings? Oh no! How about your teacher? One girl said, "There is this boy in school who says sexual things and touches my butt… How can I tell my teacher? He's always staring at my best friend's ass!" So I asked them again, who can you talk too? And they answered in unison: "You!"

So we began roleplaying how to be assertive and clear with boys who were being inappropriate. "I don't feel comfortable when you say those things. I'm only eleven and not interested in sex." They also had to be respectful because those boys could get violent. At the beginning of each new school year, the organizations that offered AIDS awareness sent home notes and consents for participation. We set up times where parents could meet me, have coffee, and find out why this older guy was teaching their daughters about HIV, other STDs, sex ed, etc. One parent showed up (over three years) in several sites. A mom who said, "No way I want my daughter involved!" Hey, she showed up! This was incredibly frustrating for me. Apathy, people with their heads stuck in the sand, fear of discussing controversial issues, whatever!

So I knew and the organizations that offered this prevention program also knew that we were on our own. Luckily, I had excellent supervision, incredibly supportive staff (the ones who knew me), and a lot of clinical experience. I also realized that AIDS awareness had morphed into sex ed, preventing sexual abuse, as well as HIV info and prevention. An interesting side note was that they remained primarily female. I ran latency-aged boys' groups, but the follow through was spotty at best. Same with the adolescent males, unless they were a "captive" audience like in a school or residential program. Younger boys had difficulty tolerating sensitive information. Maybe that's an illustration of how girls mature faster than boys. I attempted several mixed gender groups, and the boys displayed immaturity or postured in a dominating manner, and the girls became less assertive, almost submissive. And the girls were much more receptive to the info. I've often wondered, if I had been female, would the roles have been reversed? Maybe discussing sexual info with a male was too threatening for young pre-sexual boys. Maybe having a safe, nonthreatening older male was safer for the girls. Anyway, other than mixed high school aged groups, the majority of my participants were female.

The serious stuff was almost always interspersed with humor. What John Ingram Walker referred to as cosmic humor in his excellent book *Complete Mental Health*. I have much more to say about his book in a subsequent chapter. One latency-aged group asked me to clarify a word they had heard and were unsure about. My approach has always been honesty (99 percent of the time) with a range of info based on age and maturity level. Well, the word was masturbation. So I'm sitting there thinking *these little girls are gonna go home tonight... Parents are gonna ask what they did learn at the Boys and Girls Club... They're gonna say, "We learned all about masturbation!"* Ah, not good. But it was a legitimate question, and I was teaching sex ed along with HIV prevention. So I had to do my job! I felt like this was one of those times to offer basic info and not elaborate. So I said that masturbation was when you touch yourself in a private place. Silence, then, "Does it feel good?"

So I said, "Yes, sometimes."

Next question: "Can you hurt yourself when you touch yourself?"

I said, "Yes, if you do it too much or too hard." By the way, I was obviously flying by the seat of my pants.

Silence again, then another follow up question: "Do you have to do it?"

I said something like, "No, it's a personal choice."

So the group leader, Jenny, stands up and declares, "I'm not touching myself." The others follow her lead. And then they sealed the deal by forming a circle, raising and joining their hands, and declaring (in unison), "No touching the bagina!" This was both nerve-wracking and hilarious. When I filled in the staff, they were on the floor in hysterics. I did the best I could.

Since we're on the subject of masturbation, a few thoughts. Once again our society has messed with female heads and has taught them that touching themselves sexually is wrong. For pubescent boys (wink, wink), this is all part of growing up. I've done multiple groups with adolescent girls and young moms who have expressed disgust at the thought of touching themselves sexually. They've been taught that it's wrong, and I'm sure this is multigenerational. Oh, and many of these young women have never experienced an orgasm or enjoyable sex. It's always been about pleasing the guy. And they are disgusted by female pubic hair. And it's a vicious cycle, because young guys have been taught the same beliefs (about the female body and sexuality). I remember running a young parenting group when the topic of masturbation came up. Most were horrified at the thought and fairly shocked when I normalized it. I casually asked if any used sex toys, and they were shocked at that. And all these women were pregnant or had kids, so sex was nothing new. They thought about it and asked me to buy them each vibrators. I said that this was not in my job description.

All these factors were going through my mind when my latency-aged girls' group asked me to clarify masturbation. I was honest but also discreet. I just hoped that they wouldn't be traumatized by society's fucked-up messages regarding normal sexual development.

After that group, I drove to a co-ed alternative high school. With my head still twirling from the previous group, I asked this small mixed group, "How was your weekend?"

"Really weird!" said one sixteen-year-old student, with his buddy emphatically nodding his head. I asked them what was so weird about it. "We each took three of my uncle's Viagra." I had to ask what happened next. Apparently, they called their girlfriends and had sex for two hours. At that point, the girls said, "We are outta here!" and left. They added that they "never lost our erections... so I taped mine to my stomach, and Bob, his to his leg...then we went about our business." One went to school and the other went home. By then, everyone in the class was screaming with laughter (including me). The director of the program peaked through his door to make sure everthing's okay. I pulled it together as best I could and with a stern voice warned them about medical complications from Viagra. I asked them, "Do you guys...healthy sixteen-year-olds...have difficulty getting it up?"

"Oh no," they said.

So I said, "Don't ever do that again!" They promised me that this would never happen again.

As I drove away, I began to think about the content of those two groups. It was too much and I had to pull over. I was laughing so hard tears were running down my cheeks. Then I started thinking about how I must look to passing motorists. This made me laugh even harder. Gave me cramps! Once again, I thought of everything you never learned in school. And that I was getting paid for this.

The "no touching the bagina" group was with me for three years, and they provided classic moments. At one point, they structured AIDS awareness so that it was divided into three segments: talk time, exercise time, and snack time. Twenty minutes each. The verbal part came first, then exercise (singing, dancing, flipping, and cheering, since several were budding cheerleaders), and then snack. Sometimes we had pizza delivered. One day they decided to have snack time before exercise. I said, "No, no, no," and they said, "Yes, yes, yes." You guessed it: six girls sitting on desks with wastebaskets for barfing. Luckily, no one got sick. They swore they would go back to the original order of the group.

Coincidently, I ran into Jenny four years later in a short-term STAR program. She was fifteen, and this was a co-ed adolescent AIDS awareness group. When the topic of sex came up, somebody suggested that we go around the room and disclose the age when we lost out virginity. Kids who are sexually active love that topic. Well, Jenny points at me and said, "This guy scared the living shit out of me four years ago, so I'm still a virgin!" She received a lot of positive feedback. I felt good, except for scaring the shit out of her. In groups where kids and adults come and go, I always wonder about the long-term effects of counseling.

A similarly aged group provided another cosmic humor moment. Since a renovation was taking place, my group was moved to a large room packed with religious artifacts. In the corner was a sofa and several chairs. So after I told everyone to "not touch anything," we sat down and proceeded with group. Then I noticed that Emily was missing. Everybody shrugged. The group had begun in a weird way. As we settled in, two male workers carrying a tabletop casually walked through the doorway and stopped in the middle of the room. Placed the tabletop on the ground and stood at opposite ends. Just silently staring down at it. So I said, "Excuse me, this is a private group," so they picked the tabletop up, retraced their steps, and made an exit. The room had doors on either end, and they promptly entered from the other side, placed the tabletop on the floor, and stood over it. Seriously? I thought of the Three Stooges. If there was one thing about my little girls' groups, it was loyalty to the process. Before I could respond, the group alpha stood up, marched over to these two guys, and said, "This is girls' group, get the hell out of here!" They quickly left without the tabletop.

It was shortly after this that I noticed Emily was missing. Seeing the door to a storeroom was ajar, I walked over and took a peek. On the way, I heard Emily mumbling. Remember how I said that this room was full of religious artifacts? Well, Emily had cornered a life-sized model of the pope and was telling his holiness off and slapping him about the head. Laughing and enjoying it tremendously. "So, you think you're really something?" Slap, slap, slap! By now we had been joined by the other girls, who were (once again) on the ground laughing. Emily kept ranking on the pope, and I'm trying (really trying) to be a responsible adult. Fate intervened. The door opened, and the secretary walked in. Aghast is way too mild a reaction. She almost burst into tears. One of my girls slapping the shit out of the poor pope. She screamed and told us, in no uncertain terms, that we could never use this room again for group.

The adolescent AIDS awareness groups, especially the alternative high schools, usually tested me, at first, to see if I had any staying power. In one, a male student asked if he could go to the bathroom. Who am I to say no? So he went to the bathroom, snorted cat tranquilizer, and returned to his desk. He proceeded to get very woozy and slid out of his chair onto the floor. Very smooth, like he had no bones in his body. Still conscious and smiling like crazy. Did I mention that these kids had issues with drugs? So I found the director of the program and filled him in. Then the sirens and fire trucks and ambulances! They shut the school down and carted him off on a stretcher, still smiling and babbling away.

The next week I entered the room to solemn, unforgiving faces. Especially the girls. By the way, I had checked on cat tranquilizer kid and he was fine. So Corey informed me that the boy was dead and it was all my fault because I'd turned him in. Just like that! So I'm thinking, *This is the way you want to play…well, okay, here we go!* I responded with "I don't care!" Shocked silence.

Then another girl said, "You're a therapist. You have to care!"

I said, "No I don't!" then I quickly added that I did care, that I knew he wasn't dead, and that what they said was bullshit… and mean. They liked me after that.

That was one of the adolescent programs that couldn't tolerate a co-ed format. Too much triggering info for kids with raging hormones. So I alternated male and female groups, each twice per month.

As I mentioned before, with the teens I used an ABC prevention/harm reduction model. Abstinence or be monogamous and use condoms. What happened was that the longer term group members, especially the girls, took this info in and created their own harm reduction model. The fact that anal intercourse was the riskiest unsafe sex led multiple girls to say no to anal sex. More oral sex, without condoms. They had a difficult time wrapping their heads (no pun intended) around the idea of oral sex with a condom. I brought various condoms, flavored dental dams, female condoms, etc., but they fought safe oral sex. Many insisted that they would have one sexual partner (that's good!) and switch to other forms of birth control after condom usage. And several girls said that they would seek out virgins. "How would you know?" I asked.

"Oh, we'd know!" they said. I pointed out all the time that girls were more at risk in heterosexual relationships than guys, and one of the main reasons was serial monogamy. Dating someone for a while, using condoms at first, switching to, say, the pill, breaking up, and dating someone new. Then repeating the process. I still pointed out that if you have unsafe sex with only one new guy a year, in five years you're indirectly connected with everyone that they've been involved with (for ten years?). This has always tended to scare the crap out of my clients. My goal was to urge all sexually active participants to get HIV tested and demand the same of current or future sexual partners. The adolescent girls resisted confronting sexual partners about getting tested because "They will think I'm a slut, not because I'm protecting myself!" Another fucked up societal message that young girls have internalized.

In one girls' group, I described the highest risk behaviors. Multiple partners, no condom use, sex with an intravenous user, using IV drugs, oneself. As the group progressed, one fifteen-year-old got whiter and whiter. At the end of the group, she hung around and then blurted out, "I've had fifteen sexual partners… never used a condom…and at least two of my boyfriends shot drugs. Am I screwed?" I told her to get tested as soon as possible and no more unprotected sex! Every group after that I'd ask her if she'd been tested, and she kept saying that she was too scared. For four months this went on. Finally, she said, "I'll go if you accompany me." I met her at a nearby clinic and held the door for her. At that point she said she'd do it on her own. I hope that she was HIV-, but I never found out. She went home prior to my next scheduled group. Due to confidentiality issues, the group home couldn't give me her address or phone number. If I had known she was leaving, I would have given her my phone number.

I saw some kids for years but was unable to engage in a clinically appropriate termination. Some went AWOL; some got kicked out some went home; some were transferred. Violations of probation meant being sent to a more secure setting. This was unfortunate because these became very intense therapeutic groups. The schools offered more structure, whether or not the program resumed in the fall. Sometimes a new director or an unruly group or a funding issue would terminate the program. No heads up! No phone call! I'd arrive and be told, "This is the last group. Next week we have a cooking class!" So I would do my one-hour termination and the kids would be distraught. "How is a cooking class more important than preventing us from being sexually abused, or getting AIDS?" I learned to live with it, but I hated it.

One of my biggest peeves was the lack of accountability and effort by certain agencies and staff members. Plus, I did all the initial groundwork. I contacted them, explained the program, provided HIV and STD info and prevention, sex ed, sexual abuse prevention, anger management, substance abuse and systems explanation and more. All for free. Sometimes I felt like I was enabling systems. The more I did, the less they did. This was what I bitched about the most to my supervisors. But I also realized that these alternative schools, residential settings, prerelease programs, and youth service agencies were incredibly stressed. They were often crises filled with underpaid staff and high employee turnover. I waltzed in once or twice a month and ran an hour-long group. Very little pressure. Plus, because I was an outsider and not actual staff, I didn't face the same adolescent oppositional behavior. I deferred to the staff all the time because this was their program, not mine. So who was I to judge how I was treated?

I used to feel for the staff when their clients would split (figuratively) with me being the good guy. I remember walking into one female residential program and the place was empty. Only, not really. At the end of the corridor, I could hear "Fuck you...leave me alone!" One of my favorite clients, Candy, had barricaded herself in her room with all of her furniture against the door. "Fuck off...I'm not coming out!" The staff and social workers were cajoling, pleading, and gently warning her that the fire department would have to come in through her bedroom window. "No! No! No!" she kept saying. One of the staff casually mentioned that I had arrived and that it was time for group. Candy quieted down and methodically removed everything from her blocked doorway. Then she slowly walked out, down the hall, and was the first one ready for group. With a shit-eating grin that was priceless. What a ball buster! I felt bad for the pleading staff, but they knew the score.

By the way, Candy was one of my favorite group adolescents. She would enter group, outraged that "those goddamn boys want sex and won't leave me alone!" Her guidance counselor taught her an anxiety-reducing technique. Snap your fingers rapidly when agitated. So in the midst of group, while talking about "those goddamn boys," she'd climb up on her chair and begin rapidly snapping her fingers. Seemed to work pretty well because she'd end up laughing.

These adolescent girls' groups could be absolutely nuts. I realized early on that they reminded me of inpatient psychiatry, due to the zaniness and frequent lack of structure. Candy's group and the residential setting became my favorite and most intense group for several reasons. First of all, I developed a great rapport with the director and staff. They hired me to do staff training around addiction, family/systems work, holistic techniques, anger management with teens and adults. A relationship with total mutual trust. Then they hired me to provide anger management. So I began alternating AIDS awareness with anger management. Then these groups got really interesting! Some of these girls were in weekly groups with me for six months. AIDS awareness, sex ed, anger management, substance abuse prevention, healthy relationships, coping mechanisms, preventing sexual abuse, all from an ego-supportive, feminist, and systemic perspective. A lot of information. We talked about being the identified patient in dysfunctional family systems. We talked about meds, previous counseling experiences. Everything I ever learned about depressed, anxious, and angry adolescent girls contributed to these groups. And I knew a lot of them from previous school and Boys and Girls Club groups. And some were my former individual and family therapy clients. Or HIV+ clients. Full circle!

One week, we might watch an HIV-related video, have an HIV+ guest speaker, or have a condom (male and female) demonstration with one black and one white penis and a vagina demonstrator. With cherry- and pina-colada-flavored dental dams. Or teaming exercises and roleplaying. The next week would be anger management, with a watered-down version of my adult anger management groups. The most frustrating aspect for me was the lack of family systems work getting done. The staff tried, but the families resisted. The same old scapegoating process with the family in denial. Meanwhile, back in anger management, these girls were disclosing multigenerational addiction, trauma, neglect issues, being parentified, and on and on. They were getting to the bottom of what made them depressed and angry. The next logical step was family systems work, and it wasn't happening. So the focus of my group would become how to deal with the frustration of not having your family directly involved in treatment. First versus second-order change, again! I knew what was going on. Staff knew what was going on. And my clients knew after typical denial and loyalty issues. I realized that I was stirring up a lot of shit, but somebody had to do it. Otherwise, it would have been Erica or Karen or fifty other scapegoated women I've worked with.

These groups had an organic, nonlinear quality based on longevity, mutual trust, the variety of subjects addressed, and the interplay between deadly seriousness and crazy, spontaneous humor. I will never forget one powerful sequence. Same group of girls over the span of one month. It began with one of the funniest and hyper AIDS awareness groups I ever saw. One girl put a condom on her head. Another snuck up behind me and wrapped a cherry-flavored dental dam around my face. That's how I was able to describe the taste of a cherry dental dam in subsequent groups. The condom demonstration included a black and white penis. They howled when several pointed out that the black penis was much larger. Absolutely bananas group. That was one of those times that I thanked my lucky stars for the trust of the staff.

The next group was anger management with my adolescent girls having done an abrupt 180. No more fun and games! A totally depressed and subdued group with blunted affect and zero interest in participating. I wondered if they all were premenstrual. I kept this thought to myself because I always have valued my life. So we had a low-key group, which was what they obviously needed.

One week later, early on, one sixteen-year-old disclosed having been sexually abused as a child. No prompting…it just came out, then another, then another. Being a mandated reporter, I was obligated to record and report these disclosures. The problem was that they came in waves. So I paused the group after telling them that I needed a recorder. I went to staff, and one female staff member sat at the back of the room and took names, dates of alleged incidents, perpetrators, etc. Locations and family involved. I was freaked out! Luckily, it was summer, so when I drove home, I went immediately to the lake near my house and had an intense swim. Very cathartic! The next morning I got up and called the Department of Social Services. I filed eight to ten 51-As over the next three hours.

When I try to look at what happened objectively, I see the continuum in life that includes pain and pleasure, pathos and joy. And the building of trust through time and safety. Dialectics! It reminds me of when I worked in inpatient, with clients whom I had minimal "therapeutic" contact with. No 1:1 or family work. Just eating meals together, playing cards, going for walks, having a few laughs, telling jokes. Always with humor unless the situation dictated otherwise.

Prior to being discharged, two females asked to speak to me and disclosed sexual abuse. They hadn't talked about it with their primary clinician over the previous month. This was awkward because it didn't make their primary clinician feel very competent. Another client, while saying goodbye, added, "Oh, you're staff. I thought you were another patient." What a great compliment that was!

I get the whole termination/disclosure phenomenon thing about clients being freed up to talk about new issues, or as a way to hang on to the relationship, or a paradoxical element going on. But I know that it was more than that. We had created trust through humor and nonthreatening activities. It makes total sense when you consider traumatized and sexually abused females (for the most part) developing trust for a new male in their life. So that's what I think happened in my AIDS awareness/anger management group.

Which brings us to the transference issues. One girl walked into my group and basically gave me shit for one month. On a routine basis she reminded me that I was poorly trained, couldn't work with girls, knew nothing about anger management, was a closet homosexual, never shut up. Also said I didn't talk enough. Since I'd been down this road before, I just smiled a lot. Then we conducted a feedback group where each girl went around the room and offered advice. "You're funny...you have nice hair...I like your clothes...I like that you're real." Then she gets to me and begins fuming and escalating. "And you...you...ah... you piss me off...you don't help at all!" So I asked her if I reminded her of anybody. "My father, you're just like my father." And the air goes completely out of her sails.

I said, "That's a transference issue; I remind you of your dad, so you vent with me." She never raised her voice to me again. As a matter of fact, from that day on she had my back. When a new participant would get pissed at me, she'd say, "Oh, that's a transference issue, you're not really pissed off at him." Another also gave me shit for about one month. (I don't know why this process takes a month...one group a week for a month to develop trust?) Anyway, after one month she had my back to the point that she would get in the face of anyone who gave me shit. She also played pranks. She'd set me up with a new girl and then rescue me at the last moment. By the way, I explain transference and countertransference to all my clients.

This group also provided me with my favorite clinical vignette concerning adolescent girls and group counseling. During one of the AIDS awareness/sex education meetings, the alpha, a very tough sixteen-year-old, said, "We have a question for ya." So I reiterated the rules: no personal questions regarding my sex life, etc. As far as personal info, I did make some exceptions. If they asked me whether I was gay or straight, I told them I was straight. During the virginity discussions, if they asked I'd say, "I was eighteen." I hoped that this might show them that you could initiate being sexually active when older. I also said, if I wasn't dating, how much I could accomplish while being single. I always had to explain that being single didn't necessarily mean "being a player." For me, it meant not being intimately involved and focusing on other things. This always drew a few blank stares and "what's wrong with you?" comments. I've always hoped that this might offer an alternative to kids who were constantly bombarded with sexual images.

Anyway, this group reiterated that they respected and trusted me, and besides, I was the "sex" guy and the one to ask these questions too. And the questions were great! Such as:

"Can you get pregnant from oral sex?"
"Can you get pregnant from anal sex?"

"Do blue balls really exist?"

"Is semen good for your skin?"

"Why do girls queef?"

"Do blowjobs really feel that good?"

"Is it weird to have balls?"

"Where do you tuck your balls when you're not using them?"

"Does it feel that good to scratch your balls? My boyfriend says it does."

"Does it really hurt that much to get kicked in the balls?"

"Does it hurt when you have an orgasm, because my boyfriend has this pained expression?"

"How do I know if I've had an orgasm?"

What is it about teenaged girls and testicles? Perplexed and fascinated! One group fantasized about having a "dick for a day...to have sex like a guy...and balls for a day... so you could scratch your balls!" Seriously!

So I thought that I'd been asked just about everything and was stunned when she asked, "What's pussy taste like?" I'm almost never at a loss for words, but this time I was. Complete silence, with these adolescent girls patiently awaiting my brilliant answer. The group ended, and usually, they would say goodbye and race out to call their boyfriends, visit family, go for a walk. Not this time. They were fixed in their seats. The door opened, and a young female staff member walked in and asked why nobody had left. The alpha said, "We're waiting for the answer to a sex question."

The staff member innocently asked, "What's the question?"

The answer: "What's pussy taste like?"

The staff member got rattled and stays "Ah…you can't ask him that, put him on the spot like that!" Then, she exited quickly.

I was still stunned, and what came out of my mouth was "Have you ever had cantaloupe?"

Silence again, then the girls began talking among themselves. "Is this guy crazy?" More silence. Everybody was just shaking her head. Then somebody asked: "Are you saying that pussy tastes like cantaloupe and fish?"

And there was my out. I got real serious and said, "I wouldn't know about that because I'm deathly allergic to all seafood. If I eat fish, my throat closes up and I experience anaphylactic shock. Very bad. When I was a kid, relatives from out of state would visit, and everybody would chow down on lobsters and clams. I'd be relegated to beans and hot dogs." More silence... Then they offered compassion to poor old me, jumped up, and exited. Just like that! The staff apologized, even though they had nothing to apologize for. As I've said before, I'm desensitized to group chaos, and besides, this was really funny.

About one and one half years later I was running another prevention group an hour away. This was an adolescent residential program for girls with addiction issues. I noticed that one of the girls was looking at me with this sly grin, so I said, "What's up?"

She asked, "Are you the cantaloupe man?"

I said rather proudly, "Why, yes, I am." She said that she heard that story from a friend, who had heard it from someone in that group. The rest of the group was wondering just what in hell we were talking about, so I told the story. Of course, they loved it! Thus began the retelling of the cantaloupe vignette.

This ended with the teen who recognized me saying, "I don't think you were talking about flavor. I think you are talking about texture." I complimented her for her big brain.

I've already mentioned their fascination with testicles. Well, another thing I've noticed through the years is the female (and male) preoccupation with breasts. I guess it's a maternal food thing, but I can't count the number of little girls, latency-aged, teen, and adult females who could talk all day about boobs. I expected this with the adolescent boys, but I never expected the depths and extents of conversations with females. I know that a lot of it has to do with the objectification of the female body. My latency-aged girls would look down at their flat chests and just sadly shake their heads. One fall, a participant returned with a plunging blouse and cleavage. Her face was gleaming like Christmas morning. And the others just sadly shook their heads. I reassured the rest that they would develop breasts.

So, in one of my adolescent sex ed groups, I commented on how some girls were reaching puberty at an earlier age, so, subsequently, they were developing faster. Of course, they began a lengthy discussion about breasts. When I added my two cents (bigger at an earlier age), they reached into their blouses and tossed balled up socks in the middle of the room. "Oh, these ain't real."

No breast discussion is complete without a vignette from my adult women's anger management program. During a self-esteem discussion, one twenty-year-old blurted out, "I'm tired of looking like a little boy. I'm getting a boob job, so I won't be here next week." I have mixed feelings about cosmetic surgery, but it wasn't about me and sometimes I need to keep my mouth shut. So I wished her the best! Two weeks later, she was the first to arrive. She walked through the door and said, "What do you think?" She was now a full-figured young lady.

I mumbled and bumbled and said, "Ah, nice…good job!" It was, indeed, a weird moment for me.

She sat down and said that it had been an adjustment. "Like now I have to sit back from the table. And now I lose crumbs down my cleavage. I never had cleavage." The other women had arrived and complimented her on her new boobs. Then they empathized with the crumbs down the cleavage. Everyone was supportive (no pun intended). Two other participants talked about their experiences with breast implants. One member (borderline symptoms) looked at me and shook her head. Throughout the fourteen-week curriculum, she has alternated between telling me that I'm the world's greatest therapist and that she could do a better job running the group. This time, she tells me that I'm unprofessional because I was looking at my clients' breasts. I said that all they've been talking about for twenty minutes were breasts. She just sadly shook her head, while everyone else thought it was hilarious.

The next week, my client with the recent cosmetic surgery announced she was really pissed off. I asked what was up, and she said that during a meeting with her probation officer, "she was staring at my new boobs the whole time… I think she's a dyke!" Here we go again…new territory! Never in graduate school was I taught how to counsel anger management clients concerning sexual harassment with a probation officer following a boob job. Hey, but this is what I signed up for. So we reviewed the assertiveness curriculum and roleplayed. This was tricky because we were talking about her probation officer, who could surrender her and send her to jail. But it all worked out.

My other favorite AIDS awareness group was a prerelease correctional facility for fifteen to twenty adult women (ages eighteen and older). I originally targeted this facility for my program due to the multiple risk factors. Female, many women of color, prison histories, IV drug use, survivors of physical and sexual assaults. A percentage with hepatitis B and C. All the high risk for HIV factors rolled into one population. Due to the distance involved, I saw this group once a month. Initially, the director offered a cofacilitator for fear of these women being disrespectful, rude, or acting out. Nothing could have been further from the truth, I worked at that site for two years and I have never been so warmly received and treated with such respect at any other facility or program. The focus was AIDS and HIV, but we touched upon all the related issues. Addiction, sexual abuse, anger management, other STDs, family systems, and dysfunction, feministic thinking, parenting, and on and on. I talked about my girls' group... concerns and goals. I asked for advice from a maternal and parenting point of view. We discussed codependent relationships, depression, anxiety, psychotic disorders, meds, eating disorders, ADD, stimulant treatments. Healthy relationships, diet, and exercise. Many women asked if I could follow up with 1:1 counseling or family work or couples counseling. I referred several to my anger management program. A thirty-year-old who looked familiar to me announced that I had been her counselor at fifteen. I later worked with her son, also fifteen.

I loved that group! I realized that, in many ways, it was the culmination of multi-problem counseling, so I felt it was almost karmic. After the trust was established, the guards welcomed me, the staff made it a point to thank me, and the inmates asked if we could meet more often. They asked if they could donate money to pay my fee and cover the travel costs. But this was jail, and there were limitations of what could get accomplished. When the funding ended, so did my group. The sheriff's department had no funding for any outside counseling services. I just couldn't travel that far and not get paid. Saying goodbye to that group was incredibly sad. As a matter of fact, my eyes are filling up with tears as I'm writing this.

I announced that I would be leaving at the end of my next-to-last group. I have to give credit where credit is due. The director tried to get funding, right up to the end. So I arrived at my last group and began to tell them how wonderful and accepting they had been, and I couldn't speak. I looked up and saw eighteen women with their heads bowed. They couldn't speak either. Some were crying. When I left, the staff thanked me again and asked for me to return if any funding became available. I knew this was never going to happen, which was what made it so final.

Several weeks later, I was attending a July 4th fireworks display and was still moping. I was approached by an adolescent boy who had been in an alternative high school group the previous year. He asked me how I was, and I said I was bummed out because of having to terminate with ten to twelve groups. He looked at me and said, "You should just appreciate the funding you were given to run those group." Then he walked away. So who was counseling who?

Today, I still run prevention programs at six sites. A wide range of topics, with HIV/ AIDS prevention provided on a monthly basis. On occasion, I offer training to schools and clinical staff. And to think that all of the counseling and prevention work began with that one family of four in 1992.

CHAPTER FIVE

The Butterfly Effect and Counseling

I keep mentioning the butterfly effect, so I think it's time to elaborate and go back to the beginning. Approximately forty years ago, I had completed two years at a junior college and worked odd jobs to get by. I knew I had to get a college degree but was unenthusiastic about my academic fields of interest: English and History. I liked to read and write but had no idea how this would translate into a career. I applied to and was accepted at a four-year college. I arrived at orientation on a brutally hot September morning in a facility that lacked air conditioning. My plan was to major in either History or English.

Good plan! Until I approached the "History major" line and saw fifty or sixty aspiring (or perspiring) students moving at a snail's pace. That was it for the history career! I moved on to the "English major" line where there were seventy or eighty. Too hot, that ended my English career. I looked around for the shortest line and "psychology major" and with no one in line. Why not? I had taken one psych course in junior college and it was interesting. I had flunked it because I was in love for the first time and couldn't concentrate in class. I repeated it, got a C, and now I figured being a Psychology major was okay.

The faculty member who interviewed me asked me why I chose Psychology as a major, and I told him that there was no one in line and that it was incredibly hot. He got irritated and said that this was a lousy reason to make a choice. I was stubborn and signed on. By the way, he became my favorite professor for several experiential classes.

Fast forward three years. I've finished undergraduate school, am unemployed, broke, no car, and beginning to wonder who will hire someone with a BA in

Psychology and no work experience. Let me tell you, having no experience and a BA in Psych sucks! Since I had no car, I did a lot of hitchhiking. Actually, I could write a book about that because some wild shit happened! But anyway, one morning I'm hitchhiking, and this guy picks me up. We're talking about the weather and the Red Sox, and he asks me what I do for a living. "Nothing," I reply. Because I couldn't find a job. He says that there is a federally funded program through a nearby junior college that provides counseling and GED (Math, English) teaching at the local jail. How would I feel about working with inmates? Why, this is right up my alley. No counseling experience, no inmate experience, and I suck at math! Sign me up! He writes down the contact person at the college, who turns out to be my cousin. Whom I haven't seen in five years.

So my first job in the field was as a teacher/counselor at a nearby jail. There were five or six of us, and I was the only one who ever worked. Seriously! Everybody else punched in, left for the day, came back, and punched out. No respect for a gift job. When they came to review the progress of the program, I was the only one working. All the inmates confirmed this. So the program was immediately shut down. I was crushed! And then I received a glowing letter of recommendation, which led to my first job in inpatient psychiatry.

Since the title of this chapter is the butterfly effect and counseling, I think you know where I'm going with this. One definition of the butterfly effect is the phenomenon in which a small change in a chaotic system's initial state (metaphorically caused by the flap of a butterfly's wings) leads to a huge change in what follows, compared to what would have happened otherwise.

This definition comes from Steven Strogatz of Cornell University. Specifically, from his DVD course and accompanying guidebook, both entitled *Chaos*. This is an excellent program offered by the Great Courses. I would also suggest *Chaos, Making a New Science* by James Gleick (1987.) That book blew my mind, and I can honestly say that I have never thought the same since reading it twenty years ago.

I've always wondered how random events and nonlinear progression have affected my clients and counseling in general. I just never knew how to conceptualize the experience. Having a systemic perspective reinforced multiple and minute factors that never seemed to be talked about in team meetings and client reviews. I used to read straightforward case studies and think, *This is so much more complicated. There are so many factors not being addressed.* I don't think life is linear, so how can counseling be? It helps me tremendously to think this way with addiction. Relapse as part of recovery. Harm reduction instead of abstinence. Think of the butterfly effect and my educational experiences. What if there were two hundred students in line at the psych major table? What if it had been thirty degrees cooler and I didn't mind waiting? What if I hadn't been hitchhiking that morning? What if the guy who picked me up had taken a sick day or a different route to work? What if he didn't pick up hitchhikers? What if my cousin didn't run the program? What if everybody at the jail did their job, so my recommendation was generic?

I've told this story multiple times. Responses have included God stepping in with a divine response or karma or "it was meant to be…predestination!" How about a series of random events and coincidences and luck? Or a small change in a chaotic system leading to significant change.

Ernest was referred to me from a foster care placement when he was eight. Horrible sexual victimization history involving his family. I was his individual psychotherapist and family therapist for nine years. I saw him in six foster homes. He had severe PTSD, chronic depression, anxiety, ADHD, major attachment issues, and explosive tendencies. School was almost impossible, and his peer relationships were dramatically limited. He was scarred, and therapy was slow. He would have periods of growth and progress, relapses, emergency removals and new placement, assessments, and hospitalizations. Reactions to meds and borderline-like mood swings. I worked with Ernest from childhood to adolescence. In his last foster placement, he was fairly stabilized with limited success at an alternative high school. Appeared to be on the right meds. His affect was brighter, and he was more optimistic about his future. His DSS service plan included a pre-independent living placement and job training. For the first time in my nine years with him I could honestly say that there was light at the end of the tunnel. For the first time, I was discussing an appropriate termination from his current living situation.

And Ernest had an after-school job! This was a huge success because he had never been able to maintain a job. And he liked his job bagging groceries at a nearby food market. He was a chattering and sociable employee, and the customers loved him. So one day, he's bagging groceries for an elderly lady and he introduces himself. The customer says, "That's a coincidence, my grandson's name is Ernest too, and I haven't seen him for years." You guessed it! She's his maternal grandmother. They have a tearful reunion. He removes his apron and leaves with her. No more job! No more foster placement! No more meds! No pre-independent living! He was seventeen and clear about what he wanted to do. I lost contact with him and a social worker told me that he was homeless and possibly prostituting himself to survive.

Is this case study an excellent example of the butterfly effect or what? While working at his first real job, he just happens to begin talking to a family member whom he hasn't seen in ten years. And he just happens to mention his first name. Talk about the "flapping of the butterfly's wings" leading to a huge change! I had an epiphany at that point. I hadn't begun reading about chaos theory, but I began to consider all the random events that impacted my clients and families and groups. I always felt that I could never exactly describe my client's situation because it was dynamic, always shifting. And it almost never fit neatly into a diagnostic box. In team meetings, I'd think, *There is so much more going on here, I can't even put it into words*, and this was constant because my work was home based. I saw butterfly effects complicating butterfly effects. No wonder most therapists wanted no part of outreach. The pinballing precipitants and crises created cognitive dissonance and anxiety.

The saying "shit happens!" should be replaced by "shit happens all the time, from all different directions, and keeps bouncing back and forth between people." This works great with systemic theory. Say you get an angry ten-year-old kid with ADHD. Dad is alcoholic; mom is depressed. Systems work addresses where the three major characters interact and overlap. They're not seen as three separate cases, acting in a void. But while working with the family system, things are happening all the time. Curveballs all the time. I just go back to my Gestalt Foundation, the figure/ground thing, and address what is in my face. And I really believe that life is nonlinear. The Newtonian clockwork universe does not seem to apply for my multi-problem clients. Now I get it! Randomness and curveballs are not the exceptions; they are the norm. When my anger management groups dissolve (or explode?) into multiple tangents, that's the way it's supposed to be.

This is also why I'm comfortable with mixing treatment modalities instead of just seeing an individual or a couple or a family.

Think of a traditional office setting for a counseling referral. An individual adult refers himself, his child, his family, or part of his family. The presenting issues are identified from a totally subjective point of view. The precipitants and agenda are from a first order framework. (Fix my kid…fix my husband). Even family referrals are first order: identifying one person and their impact on the family system— contrast that with going into their natural environment. While being given a first order scenario, dynamics are flying around from the onset. And these dynamics are not static. Multiple issues change all the time and are interrelated. Chaos theory, simply put, means that what appears random up close has order if you view it from a distance. Systems theory talks about maintaining homeostasis. When a system becomes unbalanced, the disorder creates anxiety. So the system needs to recalibrate.

Chaos theory would say that this disordered family system has an internal structure that maintains some type of order (homeostasis, from systemic thinking). So viewed from a nonlinear perspective, it all makes sense. Crazy sense, but still sense. I remember sitting in staff and team meetings and discussing how seriously disordered families and clients always seem to attract misfortune, pain, and misery. It was due to the company they kept (true), poverty (true), self-fulfilling prophecies (true), and negative expectations (also true). And a general comfort level with chaos (interesting way to put it). And "shit seems to happen to these clients" (another way to describe the butterfly effect).

How about the butterfly effect concerning social services? The state budget necessitates cutbacks, and case workers get laid off. Disordered order continues, and inevitably, the shit hits the fan. Somebody gets killed, DSS or DCF gets blamed. The staff is overworked, and an emergency call goes out to hire more social workers. My clients have lost experienced social workers who are then replaced by younger, inexperienced social workers. How about the changing DSM diagnostic categories, new meds, and changing research-based treatment approaches? I realize that I'm kinda going on and on; but my point is, all the obvious and minor and unknown factors affect each other and have a dramatic impact on our clients. And I have not even mentioned countertransference at an individual and systemic level.

Anyway, I think you get my drift; as nuts as my anger management groups and adolescent prevention groups can be, as chaotic as multi-problem families can be, there is order within the disorder that you have to plug into to facilitate second-order change. Early in my outreach career, someone put it perfectly. Once you've gained their trust, hang on for a wild ride that could go anywhere!

Originally, that was supposed to be the end of the butterfly effects chapter. But I am rewriting this book during the Covid-19 pandemic. My plan was to write this summer. But as we all know, things have changed. Since I see clients at home or at a residential facility, this is obviously on hold due to social distancing. Social distancing: a new term we will probably never forget.

I'm not seeing clients, so I have all this time to write. My gym is closed, so I walk and walk and walk. I sleep more and have changed my diet. My TV died, so I read. While walking, I wondered about a paradoxical feature to Covid-19. People seem friendlier and more social at a safe distance. I chat with people in their yard all the time. We say take care, be safe, as well as commiserate about living in bizarro world. It feels positive! Is our need to distance making strangers closer?

This is all about the butterfly effect due to this viral bomb being dropped on us ten weeks ago. I can't even imagine both subtle and drastic changes that will come out of this. I'm keeping a Covid-19 diary, so stay tuned.

CHAPTER SIX

The Dogs of War!* Canine (mostly) Vignettes from Outreach Counseling
With apologies to Pink Floyd

Providing counseling services to families, children, and adults within their homes means contact with dogs and cats, and birds and ferrets and turtles and hamsters and guinea pigs and one baby alligator. I had an adolescent client whose boyfriend got very wasted and decided to show off in front of his equally wasted buddies. As he held his two-foot alligator, he stuck his tongue out at it. Not good! Baby alligator latched on to his tongue, and he had to go to the ER. I'm really glad I missed that. This is why you should never mix drugs and alligators.

Oh, and several horses (which frighten me due to their size) and one wolf hybrid. But mostly dogs: border collies, Rottweilers, pit bulls, labs, poodles, Dobermans, Chows, Bull Mastiffs, blind and deaf dogs, rescue dogs, and mutts of all kinds. Actually, one family I see has two boxers. One loves me and the other wants to kill me. They had to hire a dog walker during our sessions. That dog really hates me, and that has never happened before. Go figure! But more on that later. I've been bit three times: a pit bull (my fault, totally), an abused (probably psychotic) feline, and a baby ferret. Only the cat drew blood. The mama pit bull could have ripped my hand off; it was just a warning. I was overconfident, and she taught me a lesson. The ferret incident was bizarre. My sixteen-year-old client says, "Watch out for my baby ferret. It bites."

Thirty seconds later, this ten-inch furry bolt casually walks by me as I'm sitting on the sofa, turns its head slowly, eyeballs me, then launches itself through the air and gaffs on to my forearm. I scream, "Holy shit," and my client comes to my rescue.

"I warned you!" she says. By the way, I never got paid for that session, so I was bit for nothing.

I had one really close call where I think I would have been killed. I worked with a family that owned and raised Rottweilers. A big male, Ned (eighty-five pounds), was very protective of his family and was cautiously introduced to me. This was a large family with two adults and five children, and Ned would station himself on the periphery during meetings. I kept my distance and literally never touched him. At first. As time went by, Ned got closer and closer. I began to talk to him and pet him, and he began greeting me and sitting next to me. Then he began hugging me. Literally! I would sit down, and he would crawl up and put his big chest in my lap.

One day I arrived for the family session, and Ned was nowhere to be seen. "Where's Ned?" I asked. The family, somewhat guiltily (maybe projection on my part), informed me that he would no longer be allowed in family sessions.

He was no longer barking at strangers or acting intimidating and protective. So I guess the therapy was working...for Ned, anyway. He was kept in a separate room, and if the door wasn't closed, he'd sneak in, go around the couch, and sit next to me (with a guilty look on his big puss).

But my near-death experience was not with Ned. It was with his sister, Pepper. I liked them both, but to tell the truth, I think I loved Pepper. She got pregnant, had a litter of ten, and guess who was offered the pick of the litter? But my boundaries kicked in and I had to say no. I was actually a hypocrite, because several years before I had accepted two kittens from a six-year-old client. She dropped one in my lap when I was driving away. But I felt that accepting a puppy was crossing the line. I've been offered adult huskies and adult Rotties, as well as puppies. It's hard to say no when a family becomes homeless and they say that I'm the only one they would trust with their beloved pet. But this would be like assuming responsibility for their child. The relationship would never be the same. This is a therapeutic no brainer, but you do get attached. And these dogs could end up mistreated or euthanized.

So Pepper and I were very tight when I arrived for a family session. I knocked on the door, my client Annette (in the bathroom) yells for me to come in and make myself at home. I walk in and notice Pepper sleeping by the refrigerator.

She's secured by a chain, which should have been a huge red flag. But she loves me more than Ned so I never thought twice about it. I strolled on over and leaned down to say hello. What probably saved my life was her utter shock that some crazy dude would boldly approach with no apprehension. You see, Pepper was out for a ride and my client was dog-sitting for another female Rottie. So, probably out of fear and surprise, she drew back before launching herself at my smiling kisser. I simultaneously realized this wasn't Pepper and I was about to die. I sprung back, she leaped, and the chain tightened, which left her snapping in the air. If there was ever a time to crap my pants, that was the time. My client yells from the bathroom, "Oh don't go near that dog, we're babysitting, and she bites."

Meanwhile, two doors down the hall lives a friend of my client with a pit bull named Frankie. Frankie has the largest head, with gleaming teeth, of any dog that I've ever seen. That is, in proportion to the rest of his body. Remember the dog in *The Mask* after he put on the mask? I had arrived for my scheduled family session, and they were running late. I'd met their neighbor, so he invites me inside to wait. I sat down at the kitchen table, while Frankie was hunkered down by the fridge. I've learned by now not to approach strange dogs sitting by refrigerators. But Frankie is mellow looking, and I have this thing for dogs. So I ask the neighbor if Frankie is friendly and may I pet him? This guy is doing the dishes with his back to me and casually says that he will either ignore me or approach me. So I gave it a shot. I called Frankie, and he walks over and sniffs my hand. I pat his giant head. He starts wagging his tail, and I tell him how handsome he was. This eighty-pound beast proceeds to crawl up into my lap and flips over on his back. I begin rubbing his tummy, and he falls asleep. My client's neighbor says, "He likes you," and continues with the dishes.

By now, Frankie is out like a light and snoring. His head is hanging over my knee with his tongue drooping. His mouth is open, and I can't believe the size of his teeth. Never seen anything like it. This is what they mean by pit bulls! So I asked his owner if I could check out his choppers. He says, "Why not?" So I proceeded to open Frankie's mouth (gently) to have a closer look.

Then there is a knock on the door, and in walks a DSS worker I have known for ten years. We've shared many an outreach case. He just happens to be the DSS worker for Frankie's owner. (I guess that made him Frankie's DSS worker too.) I just happen to be looking down Frankie's throat, and Chris just stares in stunned silence. The best part of this story is that whenever I ran into Chris afterword, he'd remind me of when he "walked into my client's apartment and you had this pit bull upside down in your lap and you're looking at his teeth." To anyone considering home-based counseling, I wouldn't recommend doing this!

By far, the weirdest counseling dog counseling experience I ever had was with a golden retriever, Rex, in a foster home. I arrived for the session, and everyone was crying. Rex had just expired and lay on his favorite rug in front of a roaring fire. A lovely winter night by the fireplace, except for the dead family pet. So, obviously, the scheduled family session turned into a grief session. Everyone's sobbing! I'm doing the best I can to be professional and hold my shit together. Remember when Rex was a puppy! Remember his favorite toys! Really, really sad! The meeting ends and we reschedule. I shake everyone's hand and again offer my sympathy. I head for the door. Rex always walked me to the door.

So Rex jumps up, tail wagging, and escorts me to the door! Stunned silence, and then jubilation and tears of joy. Rex was alive and well! I'm thinking, *What the fuck is going on around here?* For the entire hour, he hadn't budged on his rug. I assumed he was dead, so I never checked to see if he was breathing. So was he unconscious? Was he so comfortable in front of the fire that he's like "screw you...I'm not moving for anybody." I have seen some intelligent dogs in my life and I even had the thought *is he messing with our heads?* And if he was actually...playing dead! But seriously, if old Rex was sick or injured or incapacitated, wouldn't he have staggered to his feet, wobbled over, and gamely escorted me to the door? Maybe he was just a deep sleeper. But if anyone has any info on canines feigning death during family therapy sessions, I'm all ears. Freud might have said that it was Oedipal, that Rex was having incestuous dreams involving his mother. Doggy style?

I worked with a family that had a large black German shepherd. Looked like he was part wolf due to his elongated body and long snout. During the first session, I was warned that "he's super vigilant...protective of the family...very territorial...hates loud noises and sudden movements...especially with people he does not know." Other than that, he was fine! Oh, and he had bitten the mail carrier twice. When our family meetings would get emotional, Buck would get agitated and pissed off. Now who do you suppose he would direct this to? Maybe the asshole stranger who is making people yell and cry? So when things began to get heated, Mom put Buck out on the porch. He'd just stare at me through the glass doors, and if I stared back, he'd start barking loudly.

And when I say loudly, I'm not kidding. He had by far the loudest bark of any canine or wolf hybrid I have ever heard. Deafening...like someone turned the volume up to ten when he was a puppy and never adjusted it. I never got used to it. When we eventually became buds and he'd sit next to me, he'd bark, and I'd almost fly out of my chair. And, of course, he was right by my side or had his long snout in my lap. He'd look at me with his cow eyes, and I'd massage his neck. Actually, I think this pissed off his owner that Buck warmed up to me so quickly.

One Saturday after Halloween, we were having a family meeting and the subject matter turned to #1 how much candy each child had, and #2 just how quiet and sneaky this big, loud dog could be when he raided their candy stashes. As we were talking, Buck quietly got up and shuffled up the stairs. Everyone knew he was robbing somebody's candy stash. Three stashes in three rooms. He was gone for ten minutes and then, inconspicuously, walks back down the stairs. Just stands in the middle of the room, very tense...almost at attention. He's just standing there like a statue, eyes going from one person to another. You know... how dogs can have that guilty look? Everybody ignored him, even though we knew that he knew we knew.

And then he started to drool. And I mean really drool! Until there was a small puddle under his chin. And he still hadn't moved much. Just his guilty eyes going back and forth. Finally his owner says, "Buck. Is there something in your mouth?" She goes over and opens his mouth. A fully wrapped Tootsie Roll pop with the candy end aimed down his throat and the stick end (slightly) sticking out of his mouth. One of the funniest things that I've ever seen!

One family had, well, basically a wolf. Solid white and two hundred pounds. This was the wolf/dog that you would least want to mess with. Could not be let loose, because he would kill neighborhood cats (and probably dogs). This was one scary son of a bitch! During our family meeting, he would sit stoically in the corner. I was warned to not stare at him because "wolves don't like that...they consider it a challenge." No problem there! I didn't want to die! So he'd sit there, staring at me. I'd glance over, and if I looked too long, his eyes would widen and he'd get all serious. When I arrived, he'd greet me at the door and escort me to my seat. If I had to take a leak, he'd escort me to the bathroom and patiently wait outside. Then he'd trot me back to my chair. He trained me very well! After a few months of 1:1s and family meetings, he got up and lightly walked over to me. I had a beard at the time and was leaning forward. He gently begins "fleaing" my beard with his front teeth while he's wagging his tail. His owner says, "Oh look… he's fleaing you… looking for ticks and fleas…that's wolf behavior. You are now one of the pack." Then he sat near me. But not too near! No touchy/feely stuff… just wolf respect. By the way, his teeth were much bigger than Frankie's teeth.

These dogs and hybrids were a reflection of their environment. Calm people had calm dogs; freaked-out clients and agitated households had hyper and more aggressive animals. I once worked with a very anxious and loud couple who would inevitably escalate during our sessions. A lot of crying and shouting and histrionics. When things blew up, this trembling little dog, with wide eyes, would jump up on the sofa and huddle next to me for support. If dogs could talk, he probably would have said, "For Christ's sake, would you do something?"

Brief snapshots of other dogs. Ralph greeting me at the door with lips curled and glistening teeth pressed up against the glass. A ferocious warning, right? No, actually a huge smile that greeted me every week. A long-haired mixed breed who sat in my lap during family sessions. The kids would pretend to be angry with me and make aggressive moves. This dog would stand and snarl at his own family. Very protective…of me! Don't mess with the family therapist! One day, he jumped in my lap and his face was all swollen. The family had gone away and left him with neighbors. And they had abused him! Talk about countertransference!

One Golden Retriever used to greet me at the door, grab the front of my coat in his mouth, and gently drag me in. Retrievers really do have soft mouths. A shy border collie sat next to me one day while I waited for his owner. I was rubbing her neck and found a tick. I hate ticks! I yanked it and flushed it. She immediately transformed into my best friend and would whine with joy when I arrived. A big male lab would defiantly and protectively greet me with a gruff bark. Then he would recognize me, and his face would transform into a big grin. Dogs truly smile! Then he'd bring me a stuffed animal.

If joining a resistant family, an angry adolescent, or an anxious, traumatized child is difficult, what better way than to bond with their dog. If the dog accepts me, then I must be okay. I've done many diagnostic meetings with the dog involved, and their presence (and participation) almost always relaxes the atmosphere. It usually goes like this: I arrive, and Mom or Dad immediately asks me if I'm okay with dogs. It's usually: "She's very affectionate and may jump. I can put her in another room." I immediately get tactile with their dog, and the rest is history. Then they say, "They usually don't do this with strangers." I believe this is all do to my immediately putting my hands on them.

We all know how therapeutic dogs can be. People project their emotions into them. I've done many a pet loss grief session, which is a tremendous segue to other losses (deaths, accidents, divorces, kids moving out). One latency-aged male with nonverbal learning issues always included his dog in our sessions. His dog was an absolute love who would put her head in my lap and conk out. My client would pursue her, get in her face, and she would growl and nip at him. He didn't recognize nonverbal cues, one of the criteria for his Asperger's diagnosis. Having his dog present gave me a concrete way to address his not recognizing cues.

Why did my clients often choose fearsome dogs? I think the ones who were traumatized and most insecure projected this on to their canine pets. For certain clients, their dog was their major support. And the grief work involving these pets, especially dogs. was intense and usually triggered my own countertransference. I remember one woman detailing her plans for her dog's final day. Going for a ride, sitting at his favored beach spot, his favorite dinner and snacks. Lots of tactile love and reassurance. Then holding him at the vets as he was euthanized. The therapist side of me nodded my head and complimented her efforts. The dog/human bonding side of me just wanted to sob. How does reading this make you feel? If you've ever had a loving relationship and subsequent loss of a pet, you know!

One last collie comes to mind. She always greeted me with a smile and wagging tail. She would get agitated as I prepared to leave. Then she would place herself between me and the door. As the saying goes, "man's best friend."

CHAPTER SEVEN

One Intense Week in Anger Management

At the conclusion of one of my men's anger management groups, one young participant hung around to speak to me in private. He apologized for being late, saying that he'd been dope sick and had needed some heroin to get him through the group. I reiterated the rules: that he not come to group intoxicated or high. I also urged him (again) to get into detox and rehab for his opiate addiction. He was embarrassed by the incident and insisted that he could stop on his own.

In the following group, he said that he felt good because he "had saved a life." He was shooting dope with a friend and the latter overdosed. My client got him to the hospital before he died. This led to him disclosing to the group that he was a drug addict. Another member disclosed that he was a former IV crack addict. He expressed concern for my other client, and the group turned into a compassionate and direct intervention. "What if it's you who overdoses next time and you can't be revived?"

In the same group, a homeless young male was trying to figure out how to get to my program. His only transportation, other than a train or taxi, was his mother who lived in another city. No money, no job, no car, and homeless while trying to figure out a way to complete a stipulation of his probation.

In my second men's group, during a self-esteem evaluation, one participant said that he felt better about himself "because I'm not doing or selling heroin." He also disclosed that a twenty-one-year-old female friend had just died from a heroin overdose. The group congratulated him on his recovery efforts and offered condolences regarding the death of his friend. He wasn't particularly shocked because he had lost multiple friends from opiate-related deaths.

The next night in my women's anger management, two participants (currently in a relationship) talked about being homeless and having to sleep under a bridge. Both have serious alcohol issues, with one having alcohol-related seizure history, while the other self-medicated for a panic disorder. The latter obviously needed meds, but getting a prescription was difficult due to her addiction history. Both had recently been in detox, and I urged them to go back. As the group concluded, one stayed so as to explain why she was under the weather. I thought she was dope sick or had the flu. I had noticed her symptoms during the group and commented about them. No, actually she was experiencing the side effects of PEP, or post-exposure prophylaxis, which is used to prevent HIV infection after possible exposure. While in an alcohol-related blackout, she was raped. Since she had no idea who raped her, the PEP treated was implemented. This treatment has to be initiated within seventy-two hours of the exposure to the virus, and the meds are taken daily for one month. There is no guarantee that the PEP treatment will work, and the closer the person gets to the seventy-two-hour mark, the greater the likelihood that it will not be effective.

A homeless alcoholic with a seizure disorder, raped during a blackout by a man who may be HIV+. (Or have an AIDS diagnosis, hepatitis B or C or who knows what else.) So over an eight-day period I saw sexual violence, opiate addiction, grief from a heroin overdose, HIV, alcoholism, homelessness, depression, unemployment, and poverty. And remember, this is an anger management program (usually probation mandated).

CHAPTER EIGHT

Anger Management: An Eclectic Approach

As the title states, "an eclectic approach." By that I am referring to a mixed modality and subject approach to address second-order systemic changes. First-order would include the participants for a probation referral. Domestic charges, road rage, physical and verbal altercations resulting in an arrest. As you've figured out by now, that's not my focus. Anger management techniques are part of the curriculum. But I want to address underlying issues that trigger the participants.

Which brings us to two case studies: Rick and Joanee. We begin with Rick, a forty-year-old male referred to anger management from probation, with the precipitant having been an assault and battery involving his girlfriend. Admitted to having slapped her as well as pushing a grocery bag into her. He had been physical several times, so he was incarcerated for a short time and sent to my group. He was also court ordered to attend a batterer's group, which was forty weeks. Batterer's group and anger management simultaneously. He was an hour away from the batterer's program and a half hour away from mine. He had limited access to a car. Most of the time he juggled train schedules.

Rick presented as thin and disheveled, with a slurred push of speech[1]. He did sound intoxicated or manic. Minimized the extent and effect of his aggressiveness with his girlfriend. This concerned me and made me glad he was also in a batterer's program. He fit the profile due to repeated behavior and minimizing. He did have remorse, which was significant. He also presented with multiple cuts and bruises. Said that he fell a lot but also minimized that. Now I

---

[1]Push of speech is a rapid, pressured speaking pattern that can be attributed to mania, anxiety, or substance intoxication.

was thinking that he was a drunk who fell a lot. Very intelligent, with a quick wit. Labile in his affect and quick to explode. Rick's major complaints were his girlfriend (with whom he lived) and the latter's mother who lived on the first floor. Sounded like a volatile triangle, with all three triggering each other. All three were disabled and pooled their SSI to pay the mortgage, some type of government assisted mortgage that I never understood. Rick said he had had serious alcohol issues, which were now under control. He denied any active substance problems but would nod off in my group. And he'd keep showing up with new cuts and bruises. Said that he had major sleep issues and took meds for lifelong anxiety. I've only heard this about four million times, so I figured he had addiction issues with benzodiazepine meds or opiates. In my groups, they go together like bacon and eggs, but he kept saying, "No, no, no, drugs not an issue."

When he was not falling asleep or explaining his latest injury, Rick was an awesome group participant. He liked the curriculum, loved the group process, and thought I was great. He also enjoyed his batterer's group—very unusual—while still insisting that he WAS NOT A BATTERER! Just hated the travel logistics.

As is the case with all my adult groups, I point out the rash of domestic incidents that result in men and women being court ordered to attend. At the same time I point out the lack of couples counseling reported. Makes no sense to me, so I URGE THEM TO THINK ABOUT IT when they finish the program. So Rick goes home and tells Donna that they need couples work and that I should provide the counseling because I have all this experience, plus "he's a funny bastard." He insists that she'll like me and points out that transportation will not be an issue because I go to them. I remind Rick that I don't accept insurance and he runs an amount by Donna, who says they can handle it.

I ask Rick if he wants to wait until he completes my program and/or the batterers' group before meeting as a couple; he says no, they're ready to go. He reminded me what I had said about the general need for couples work. Says that his issues with Donna are ongoing and immediately need to be addressed, so here we go!

The first two issues that come up are number one, his falling and getting injured allegedly due to his overuse of over-the-counter cough medicine; and number two, his history of getting physical with Donna. Other issues include his volatile love/hate relationship with Donna's mother, police being called, and his arrest record. Rick still minimized the first two, which concerned me. What became immediately obvious was the triangle involving all three and how enmeshed and mutually dependent they were on each other. Donna was a brittle diabetic who had hypoglycemic crises (usually at night) and said that Rick had saved her life several times. She had limited mobility due to "frozen shoulders" and was awaiting a surgery date. She also was legally blind. When I asked her how limited her sight was, she said that at four feet, she could see my face but no distinct features. She was legally disabled and lived off her own disability as well as Rick and her mother's disability. Since her house was a duplex, she also had a tenant.

Donna's mother had multiple inoperable tumors and was basically immobile. She was housebound and depressed, with some type of panic disorder. She was medicated for the anxiety, but her depression was worsening. Donna maintained that she "would never put my mother in a nursing home no matter how bad it gets." Rick and Anne (Donna's mother) were enmeshed in an intense and emotional roller coaster. When the shit hit the fan between her daughter and Rick, Anne would encourage Donna to call the police and kick him out. When things were quiet, he was a major support.

Donna spent her days going up and down the stairs, caretaking for whoever was the most anxious or depressed or who had had the most serious fall. Her brother and sister-in-law lived ten minutes away but had nothing to do with either Donna or Anne. It seems that at one point, while under the influence, Rick had threatened Donna's brother. So they cut off all contact due to no remaining loyalty to Rick. This was a major depressive issue for Donna, but even more so for Anne who had no contact with her grandchildren. Remember, they were only ten minutes away! Donna added that both adults were alcoholics and not dependable. Anne's granddaughter was described as having severe cognitive limitations and she was forbidden to visit. When I had first met Rick, he had described his family situation as "a fucking mess." He was right.

So what did I see with my new anger management participant, a "recovered" alcoholic with over-the-counter substance addiction issues? Either falling asleep, or falling down, with labile affect. Explosive and agitated. An anxiety disorder or rebound anxiety from the meds. Probably a little of both. Maybe bipolar disorder

(II) due to the extreme depressive swings that both he and Donna described. A vague and intense relationship with his own mother. ("She was fucking crazy!") His memories of his mother were fuzzy, but she sounded psychotic and violent. That made sense considering the volatile and attached-at-the-hip relationships he had with Donna and Anne. All three totally got this dynamic, saying that the women represented the mother figure Rick never had. My thought was *Get this guy on some prescription meds.* Prescribed meds from a real doctor to treat his anxiety. And a long-term sleep disturbance. Up all night doing crossword puzzles and totally exhausted during the day. Hence the falling down. Donna said that his behavior was up and down based on "those damn cold pills." He sounded like an addict when she brought this up, minimizing the effect and blaming Donna. Couples, family, and individual (for everybody) issues up the ying-yang. I sorted them out and addressed each one as best I could. They came in waves! Everyone resisted other counselors because, surprise, they had major trust issues.

My kind of case! But I was also juggling roles and responsibilities. I was working with the couple to address systemic and family issues. I was an advocate for Donna because Rick had a history of violence and she needed to be safe. I was also Rick's anger management counselor and advocated for him as well. Donna would call me, freaked out, and I would ask her if she was safe. If not, she should call the police and let the chips fall as they may. (Sorry, Rick.) She wouldn't do this for three reasons. She herself was an adult child who was locked into her caretaking role. Secondly, she (correctly) realized that his medication issue would not be addressed if he was in the clink. And financially, she needed his SSI to help pay the mortgage. Donna's biggest fear was she and her mother being homeless.

During the course of treatment, two incidents occurred, and Rick was arrested. The second incident resulted in his being incarcerated for one month. Donna went back and forth between relief that he was gone and fear of being homeless. She was also worried about his physical and mental concerns not being properly addressed if he was in jail. Talk about codependent family systems! We agreed that upon his release, Rick would stay at a nearby shelter. He could visit and stay for dinner. We could continue to work on the family issues without the pressure of him being in the house. He would continue with his groups and was in the process of hooking up with a psychopharmacologist for meds. Rick realized that the current situation wasn't working and wholeheartedly agreed with the plan.

Of course, the codependency immediately kicked in. Donna allowed him to move in during his first visit. Her rationale was "that he's fine if he's not doing those goddamn pills." We resumed the couples work. Rick was now court ordered to see a shrink, so the issue once again became transportation. Taking the train, paying for a taxi, borrowing Anne's car. Neither Anne nor Donna drove, so Rick providing the driver, Anne the automobile amid all the fighting which was an additional conundrum. I used to think, *Jesus Christ...can this get any more complicated?* Then I'd remind myself that I chose to do it this way. I could be seeing Rick once a week in group, and none of the most important stuff would be getting addressed. So, suck it up and do your job!

Upon his release from jail, Rick did well for about two weeks. Probably because he had no access to "those goddamn pills" while he was in jail. He began to stay up all night, again, falling, and was moody and belligerent. He went back and forth with the pills being an issue. We continued twice a month as Rick finished up his anger management requirement. Said that he loved the group even though it was a pain in the ass to get there.

In one of our meetings, he announced that he wanted his and Donna's relationship to be "as roommates" with no further sexual intimacy. Donna felt that the five years that she'd put into the relationship "were all a waste" and that she could have been with someone else. Rick said that he still loved her, but that "the spark was gone." He couldn't move out for financial reasons and his fear to leave Donna alone due to her numerous medical issues. So they would continue living together with limited (hugging) physical contact. As time went on, he would give her mixed messages about intimacy. For example, he wanted to lie in bed and snuggle but without sex. She felt like she needed physical distance (no snuggling) to be able to live as roommates.

So I arrived at one meeting and Donna announced that she had started dating "a gentleman who has liked me a long time and took me to dinner." Rick was fine with it. I asked him what it would be like if Donna brought this guy home, and he said he'd get used to it. They were now living in separate bedrooms. Donna still maintained that she wanted to be in an intimate relationship with

Rick, but he had made his choice. Rick was about to finish his batterers' group, and his probation officer had found a psychiatrist to medicate him. He finally admitted that he would be better off without any self-medicating. He was told that he needed to see a therapist in order to see the doctor (agency policy). And he agreed! Which was huge due to his trust issues. I had suggested this at the onset of treatment and he flatly refused. Now, with his groups finished or nearly finished, he could have his own 1:1 psychopharm person, and I would work with the couple. I also asked him to think about NA meetings due to his substance hx and how well he did in groups.

Meanwhile, downstairs, Anne's mental and physical health were deteriorating. They had worsened dramatically in the three months I had known the family. Donna was worried and even more exhausted. I met with Anne twice and urged her to get a home health aide and a therapist. She resisted the home health aide due to negative experiences with a particular service. The stress with her mother and Rick were exacerbating Donna's fragile blood-sugar situation. One time when I arrived for a couples meeting, she was nearly comatose. Sitting up, barely responsive, with Rick having her sip sugar and water. I urged Rick to call an ambulance. She wasn't responsive to me at all. I'm thinking, *Holy shit...this is it!* Rick was very tender and kept reassuring her that she'd be okay. Said that this happened all the time, and he often stayed awake to make sure she had sugar and water on hand. Donna slowly came around and looked fine within twenty minutes. She reminded me that Rick had saved her life a number of times.

At this point they are not a couple. Co-tenants with boundaries around physical contact, eating meals together, chores, etc. This was actually forcing Donna to change her codependent behavior. She was insisting that Rick make his own appointments, call his probation officer and new shrink as well as contact me if he was having a hard time. This was new behavior, actually second-order change. Donna had always resisted letting Rick be more independent. He would complain and act helpless, learned dependency. And she'd be exhausted from everything. She also stopped accompanying Rick to court and felt horrible about that. He was being weaned. At the same time, though, Anne was getting worse.

Anne had two episodes that required emergency hospitalization. One of these included psychiatric care that finally gave her an avenue to talk about

Donna, Rick, and her estrangement with the rest of her family. Talk about family dysfunction. Anne's daughter-in-law worked in the same hospital and wouldn't acknowledge Donna when she came to visit. Anne was discharged from the hospital and given home health care. But she was very ill, depressed, anxious, and utterly hopeless. We had two family sessions with the hope that Anne would agree to see her own therapist. Her prognosis was terrible. I assumed that at some point she would be hospitalized and not return home. This reinforced Donna's thinking that Rick had to stay. If her mom passed and Rick left, "I'll be blind and disabled and living on the street."

So, now I'm doing couples counseling with two people who are not really a couple. Donna still dated, but wanted to resume an intimate relationship with Rick. He actually was comfortable with the relationship and looked good. The boundaries were set, so, of course, what happens next? Maybe paradox? Or both Donna and Rick feeling a sense of relief that Anne was under better medical care? Or Rick finally admitting that he had an active addiction issue with over-the-counter meds, and that when he used, it fucked everything up? And also admitting that any self-medicating would complicate treatment when he saw his new psychiatrist. All this insight and acceptance, and it only took one year!

Anyway, they were now having sex again and cuddling. Donna had renewed hope for their relationship. Rick wasn't so sure, but he was enjoying the renewed intimacy. He would prefer that they remain roommates with benefits. The honeymoon lasted for about a week, then Donna called me and complained about Rick using. He was up all night, falling, and was nasty to her. I urged him to enter detox and think about a rehab plan. He insisted that he didn't need detox because he suffered no symptoms when he stopped taking the meds. Said that his sleep patterns went back to normal almost immediately.

Rick had an appointment in one month to begin individual counseling and finally be prescribed something for his mood disorder. I still thought he was bipolar II with anxiety, bouts of depression, and hypomania. His anxiety increased, as did his self-medicating. We were meeting every other week, when Donna called me to let me know that "Rick is dead." Said that he was having an anxiety attack and took some meds. Went into the bathroom and she heard a BANG. When she tried open the door, his body was wedged between the toilet and the door. She called

911, and Rick was transported to the hospital, where he was pronounced dead. Apparently, an anxiety-related heart attack. I wondered about an overdose.

Donna immediately voiced concern that he would be "placed in a pauper's grave" because they had no money for funeral arrangements. No burial insurance...nothing! She sobbed on the phone, saying that "he'll be in an unmarked grave." She also lamented the fact that Rick was never medically treated for his anxiety or mood disorder. We continued meeting with the obvious focus on her loss and a support network. We also kept in phone contact. Her brother and his family remained uninvolved. No phone call, no consolation. Her niece did resume visiting. I referred Donna to a bereavement group and suggested she talk to her physician about meds.

Unbelievably, two weeks later, Anne had a medical emergency and was rushed to the hospital. She died on the way. Donna called, in shock, saying, "Rick and my mother in two weeks...how can I keep my house and dogs?" The only silver lining in this clusterfuck of a situation was that her brother contacted her and helped with Anne's arrangements. Sometimes I think "clusterfuck" should be in the DSM diagnostic manual. Anyway, I remained in contact with Donna by phone.

Just another referral to my men's anger management group! Obviously, I'm being factitious. But the scary thing is that this was one client who trusted me enough to help him address the multiple underlying issues in his life. I think that a traditional anger management group would have identified stressors and taught healthier coping mechanisms. Rick would have learned techniques for controlling his emotional outbursts. But let's be real! Rick's situation was about substance abuse, childhood trauma, attachment issues, domestic violence, codependency, family problems, multiple medical concerns, poverty, long-term caretaking, enabling, and scapegoating. Oh yeah...and anger management.

I have a lasting memory of Rick. In his final anger management group, he helped introduce the program to new participants. Reluctant, court-ordered skeptical guys. Rick eloquently explained what they would get out of the group if they made the effort. Said that I "was a good guy and a funny bastard." He had my back.

Joanne was referred after serving time for an assault and battery involving her mother. She was told by her probation officer that further charges would result in two years imprisonment. Most people convicted of an assault were automatically referred to some type of anger management. Joanne initially disclosed that she had a history of alcohol and prescription drug abuse and dependency. She was freaked by the threats of additional jail time.

The real issue for Joanne was that she was a thirty-year-old adult child living at home in an alcoholic family system. And self-medicating with drugs and ETOH. Her mother was a chronic alcoholic (in denial) who would quickly display mood changes while becoming verbally and physically abusive when intoxicated. Joanne's father was physically incapacitated and subject to her mother's alcohol-fueled behavior. She was afraid for her father and felt she needed to be at home to protect him. Joanne's sibs had their own homes while insisting that she exaggerated the drinking and aggression. They maintained that Joanne could handle the situation. Her sibs had minimal contact—which was good for them, bad for Joanne. Everyone bought booze for mom.

The most recent precipitating event was an alcohol-fueled argument that led to Joanne calling the police—as her mother was biting her! The police responded, and her mother immediately showed them the bruises on her arms from being restrained. The mother denied being physical. Joanne was subsequently arrested and charged with an assault and battery on an elderly person.

After five minutes (literally) of knowing Joanne, I said, "You gotta get out!" This was a no-brainer. What was also obvious was how stuck she was. Alcoholic mother, father needing protection, designated as the only caretaker by her sibs, being unemployed and dependent on her parents for a place to live. I explained the concept of family homeostasis, that to keep the system in balance, she needed to remain as primary caretaker. To enable her mother to not have to address her alcohol dependency. To enable her sibs to not have to be more hands on. By remaining within the system, she would solidify her identified patient/scapegoat role. And her self-medicating would make it harder to leave or address the issues. I explained the concepts of first- and second-order change. The latter would shake up the system. I urged her to seek employment and find her own place. She could then support her family at a safe distance. Joanne's group was small, and she and I had 1:1 time to address her issues.

She was clearly afraid of leaving her father at the hands of her mother. The latter was fine until she began drinking wine at noon. Joanne described a schizoid relationship with her mother. In the morning they had coffee and pleasant conversation. As the afternoon progressed, the conversation became darker and nasty. It also became crystal clear that Joanne's confidence was eroded concerning independent living skills. She hadn't worked in years, after having been successful. This is long term codependency and learned helplessness due to family, being in the criminal justice system, and addiction.

Joanne was also terrified of her probation officer, or specifically, that her probation officer represented her ticket back to jail. Joanne asked that I contact her PO to confirm her participation in my program. I contacted her and asked her to advise Joanne on how best to protect her father, seek help for her mother, etc. This was new information for her probation officer. Prior to our conversation, Joanne was an elder abuser with substance abuse issues. I added that I was urging our mutual client to find a job and move out as quickly as possible. Joanne had never talked about this with her PO for fear of her mother spinning it into further assault charges.

This case is an excellent example of first- versus second-order change. First-order work would focus on Joanne's anger with her mother and her substance issues. Anger management, AA, possible meds, etc. But they would not address her codependent role in an alcoholic family system. Protecting her father, involving other family members, finding a strategy for her mother's alcoholism, becoming less dependent on her parent. These are second-order issues which are masked by first-order concerns.

Joanne finished anger management and received her certificate. She had learned some coping skills and anger management techniques. She requested follow-up individual counseling, which we began. She began looking for work and an alternative living situation. I suggested family therapy prior to her moving out as a way to ease the transition. She was incredibly nervous about her mother being involved in her therapy. Instead, we met individually for several months with the focus on her own sobriety, exercising, eating better, avoiding confrontations with her mother, avoiding the latter if she was intoxicated, and fulfilling the terms of her probation. We also discussed employment possibilities, living situation options, and having her sibs being more involved in her parents' care. She had one serious benzo and ETOH incident and then became sober. We cut back on our individual sessions due to her stability. I continued to strongly urge Joanne to find another living situation because her mother was not changing at all. One option was renting a room from another family member.

Approximately one month after our last session, I picked up the newspaper and found her name in the police log, arrested for elder abuse. She was imprisoned! I was saddened, but not surprised. I knew that as long as she was living at home, the whole thing could blow up. And it did.

These two vignettes do not have happy endings, especially for Rick and his family. My hope is that Joanne finished her sentence and made significant changes in her living situation. I may hear from her again and would gladly pick up where we left off. Ideally, we would have included her mother, father, and sibs in systemic work. But she insisted that her mother wasn't healthy enough. This was probably accurate due to her mother's level of addiction and denial. Both Rick and Joanne did a tremendous amount of work with me. This work began by building trust in groups and moving on to address systemic and individual factors. I see approximately 10 percent% of my anger management clients in follow-up services. If it were up to me, I'd see everyone in short- term individual, couples, or for family therapy.

A final word on my frustration. I strongly urge clients with addiction issues to attend Alcoholics Anonymous or Narcotics Anonymous. Statistically, they have the best chance for sobriety, especially if they have a sponsor. Clients already involved are usually enthusiastic about continuing. Others resist with the most frequent complaint being "hearing stories makes me want to use."

My other frustration is after being detoxed (usually seventy-two hours), clients deny longer term rehabilitation. Really bad idea! Especially for opiate addicts. They have to separate themselves from other addicts, substance availability, and triggers. Otherwise, it's all limited, first order success.

CHAPTER NINE

Thoughts About Anger Management

When I began doing adult anger management groups, I pictured pissed-off men and women resisting the process. What I've seen are repeating themes, problems, and precipitants. These have included:

1. Substance abuse and addiction, multi-generational alcoholism, long-term benzo and opiate addiction, misuse and dependency on prescription drugs, heavy marijuana usage, nicotine addiction, self-medicating for psychiatric disorders and physical problems, an escalation of use due to increased precipitants, a secondary addiction with rationalization ("I used to shoot dope...I've been clean for ten years...now I drink fifteen beers a day...but I'm not shooting dope").

2. Codependency, long term, with deeply enmeshed families and couples. Especially the women's group. Long-term caretaking with the women (and men) stuck in enabling relationships. This caretaking and enmeshment may not even be substance related. Could be due to extreme and untreated menial illness or physical incapacitation. They kind of get it, but they really don't due to family pressure, long-term expectations, a twisted boost to their self-esteem, and limited options. Think Joanne!

3. Negative comments and poor results reported from previous counseling experiences. Or no counseling experiences. Or long-term individual, group, or residential counseling experiences. The long-term effect ("I've been seeing a counselor since I was nine years old") results in burnout and extreme negativity.

From a systemic point of view, this makes sense. The identified patient is referred for individual counseling (first order), and since no systems work occurs (second order), other first-order alternatives like meds, a group home placement, foster care, a new 1:1 therapist are tried. Minimal couples and family work is almost always the case. For the individuals who have been the focus and in treatment all their lives, there is an almost institutionalized aspect. They assume responsibility for all the family problems—which exonerates everyone else. This also reinforces their aberrant behavior. Is this a great example of a self-fulfilling prophecy or what?

4. Long term domestic violence with an acceptance of corporal punishment. It's that identified patient/self-fulfilling prophecy dynamic. "My father threw me down the stairs and I broke my leg…I deserved it… I was a little shit!" Current domestic violence exacerbated by ETOH and drugs. I am emphatic to both men and women that "nobody deserves to be hit" in relationships. With the men, it's this macho bullshit theme that says "she's little…I'm strong and tough…I can take a punch…I'm no pussy." It's obviously a terrible precedent to set. Or a protective/enabling parent who doesn't want their teen to have a record, be placed in the system. One participant described a miserable marriage which created a dysfunctional triangulation with an assaultive fifteen-year-old daughter. Showed us scars where he had been stabbed. He and his wife could never agree on what action to take. The daughter was only violent to him. When he finally restrained her, she called the police and showed them her bruises. He was charged with an assault and battery, received a continued without finding, and referred to my group. They wanted to send him to a batterers' program, but he had no previous record. Prior to beginning group, he and his wife split up. He got his own apartment, and guess what? His daughter stopped all violence towards him. All violence after years of violence. I love systemic stuff!

5. Big time gender issues! Women who don't trust men and say "they're all dogs!" Men who don't trust women and feel victimized by the legal system (as men). Long term misogyny and objectification of women. This is obviously nothing new, but the depth of it is upsetting and slightly maddening. It makes me think *how can we work through any of this bullshit if women are still thought of as*

lesser than? Really upsetting! Men lament that "women have all the rights," and feel defeated as soon as they enter the court. Think that the only alternative is to move to a less liberal state. I remind every group that women and children have to be protected, because, historically, they were not. Infidelity is a huge trigger. But this, too, has a gender influence. Both cheat and openly discuss it in their groups. But the men rationalize this behavior as a biological necessity. The women are more passive aggressive in general, but they act this out sexually. The sexual acting out seems more ego driven for the men. For the women, it's just a sexual encounter or the beginning of a serious relationship. Regardless of gender, cheating pisses them off equally. The women report getting violent with their men. The men get violent with the other guy. And don't get me started on jealous exess (especially women). Inflamed by social media. A quick vignette: Annette was referred to anger management following a short jail sentence. This was preceded by an appearance in court where she and her boyfriend's (really) jealous ex ended up rolling around on the courthouse floor in front of the judge. They frown upon this behavior! So both ended up in jail; plus Annette was given a no-contact order. Upon release, her boyfriend's ex began harassing Annette by phone and text. She could do this because the no-contact order only went one way. After days of verbal abuse, Annette called her and left a "fuck off." The ex immediately called the police, and a warrant was delivered to Annette for her violating the restraining order. By the way, this kind of thing happens all the time (at least with my clients). Annette comes to my group sobbing, sits down, freaks out, stands up, and puts her fist through the wall. All the way up to her elbow! Things turned out okay because she kept all the messages. When she went to court, the judge scolded the ex and the no-contact violation was subsequently dropped.

6. Overzealous use of prescription meds, often with ETOH, marijuana, and other prescription drugs used in an illegal manner. Long-term prescribed usage (i.e., amphetamine type for ADD/ADHD, along with chronic alcohol and marijuana). The effect of the prescription meds has to be compromised. Long-term methadone maintenance with other benzo and ETOH use. Most clients say that they want to be tapered, but their lifestyles and addictive personalities have them as addicted to methadone as their original opiates of choice. I also see people who, I

believe, are misdiagnosed and on the wrong meds. Bipolar instead of ADHD or, at least, bipolar and ADHD. I refer them back to their physician and suggest a discussion about their diagnosis. Problem is that they are dependent (physically and mentally) to their Xanax and insist that they have an anxiety disorder.

7. Multi-problem scenarios. Working with multi-problem families in their homes, chronic addiction and HIV cases, along with inpatient cases have prepared me for what I see in anger management. Think Rick! The Gestalt approach helps because the pathology comes in waves. The referral is usually simple: domestic charge, probation, continued without finding. Then the floodgates open. Addiction, domestic violence, long term codependency, health issues, serious mental health issues, poverty, homelessness, parenting problems, marital issues, sexual abuse, incest, rape, severe relationship issues, single-parent and blended family issues, biased court systems, unethical police, racism, discrimination, and sexism. Since my adult anger management groups are free, I often see people who are currently not engaged in any other treatment. No counseling, no meds, no AA or NA. The only reason they show up is because it's free. Being court ordered doesn't hurt either! Anyway, these people are in need of multiple services, and I consider my groups a safe starting point.

Sometimes I break out the old social readjustment rating scale (copyright 1967, Pergamo Press, Inc.). This addresses life changes and rates each change on a scale of 0 to 100. For example, a minor violation of the law is given 11 as a scale of impact. The highest life change is "death of a spouse," which is given a value of 100. One participant looked at that and said, "That depends on whether you love or hate your spouse." Good point, kind of creepy, but valid. The social readjustment rating scale is going on 50. It's another technique for addressing stressors and coping mechanisms. I ask my clients to review the list, comment on the life changes and values, and then come up with their own stressors and point values. I only use this in anger management. So the responses are biased from a group of adult men and women who usually are court referred and perceived to have some type of issue with anger.

As with "death of a spouse," "divorce" (given 73 points) always draws a few chuckles. Then they begin to consider aspects of divorce. Child custody, child support, alimony, court, lawyer fees, having to leave your own house, worries about children. The discussion goes from jovial to serious very fast. As previously mentioned, the men almost always feel victimized by the legal system. I hear things like "The women always get the house...my house...and custody of the kids...especially if the judge is female." People almost immediately say the death of a child should be at the top. (Death of a close family member is given 63 points.) They also question how a divorce or marital separation could be rated higher than the death of a close family member.

Many of the stressors are seen as relative. Marriage, which is given 50 points, could have low or high stress based on the perceived success of the marriage. Same with divorce. "Change to a different line of work" is given 36 points. This could mean a career boost with better pay, or a devastating career loss due to layoffs or injury. This has applied to my men's anger management groups, especially where a career abruptly ends due to unforeseen reasons. Like the aspiring martial artist who was hit by a drunken driver and lost his arm. In these situations, I almost always see increased affective symptoms and self-medicating substance use. And PTSD. My clients look at death of a close friend (37), compare this to death of a close family member (63), and then point out that their friends are often closer than their family. In one group, two guys were going through a protracted family inheritance lawsuit. They each gave it 80 points and placed it right below the death of a loved one. Another group member nodded and said that his experience with family members contesting a will was devastating. Christmas is way down toward the bottom of the scale and is given a 12. Everybody looks at this and says, "How can Christmas be at even a 12?" They think about the stress level they feel, expectations, cost, and family bullshit, and say that it should be much higher. Any clinician will tell you how stressful the holidays are for their clients. Limited finances in a materialistic society, feigned civility with relatives they can't stand, sadness around loss, memories of childhood trauma. All made more volatile with alcohol. Watch that recent *Saturday Night Live* clip of a Thanksgiving dinner and tell me if it doesn't resonate. One of the more poignant stories from my women's group was the twenty-year-old, scapegoated family member who described how traumatic Christmas dinner was for her. I saw her before and after Christmas. She dreaded going but felt she had to make an appearance. Came back saying she'd never go again because when presents were exchanged, there was nothing for her. And nothing said about it! When she reacted in an emotional manner, she was reminded that "this is why you're on meds and enrolled in anger management." Her group was supportive. We urged her to take control and limit her participation in the future. Be cautious…spend time with her niece and nephews. If she didn't make an appearance at all, she'd be blamed for that. Merry Fucking Christmas!

"Trouble with in-laws" is given a value of 29 points. Everyone just looks at each other and falls on the floor laughing (so to speak.) "Trouble with boss" is given 23 points. This is a huge issue for some people. Plus, the list should have "trouble with other employees." One guy looked at "change in living conditions" (25 points) and asked how that could be applicable since he was homeless. He added that the scale of impact would depend on the season he was homeless.

Some groups took this exercise seriously and, as a group, came up with a "readjusted social readjustment scale." I put in my two cents' worth. Everyone agreed that there should be a range (say, 10 points to simplify things.) At the top of the list (90–100) was the death of a child, parent, sibling, spouse, close relative, or best friend. People also brought up the death of a renowned or beloved figure. It doesn't appear to be the same, but think about JFK or John Lennon. How about 9/11 or the Boston Marathon bombings or the Columbine shootings? These are obviously events involving groups of people, but can't they be as traumatic as a loved one's passing? All I know is, after 9/11, I had acute traumatic stress symptoms for approximately one month. How about the ongoing fear of terrorist acts? Food for thought!

"Chronic illness or terminal illness of self or a loved one" was given 80 to 90 points. I threw in "chronic addiction: ongoing usage and relapse of self, loved one." My clients gave that a range of 70 to 80. "Sexual abuse of a child" was given 80. While "sexual abuse and or physical abuse of self" was given a 75. "Divorce with complications" ranked a 65. "Divorce with minor complications" was given a range of 25 to 45. What do you think "imprisonment" was giving for point value? The widest range mentioned: 40 to 90. So either as bad as the death of a loved one, or a minor irritation. "Legal issues in general" and "probation" had a similar range. "Loss of employment" also had a fairly wide range: 20 to 60.

After participants introduce themselves and describe the precipitants for being referred to anger management, I have them list stressors and coping mechanisms. Healthy coping mechanisms! The latter are often nonexistent, replaced by ETOH, smoking, and drugs. As I've mentioned before, "anger problems" run a distant second to the recurring stressors and problems. And everything has complicating factors. We have an aging society, so caretaking for an elderly family member is a noted stressor. Especially for the women. They're angry because they have been left with the sole responsibility and feel guilty that they're angry. And family systems is interwoven and long term. The adult child who is expected by her sibs to be the live-in, the caregiver for their mother with advanced Alzheimer's disease. Or the twenty-four-year-old who cared for her father who put a shotgun in his mouth, blew off the side of his head, and lived. And, by the way, he had molested her when she was a little girl. On a stress level/really pissed off scale of 0 to 100, maybe she was a thousand?

But we do get to anger in my anger management groups. Cognitive and behavioral techniques, assertiveness training, conflict resolution, fight or flight, hormonal releases, and diaphragmatic breathing. And exercise. And diet. Counseling and less booze. You get the picture. There is one ironic or paradoxical twist to the process of my anger management groups. People come in pissed off and denying any anger issues. At some point, my approach leads them to blurt out, in frustration, "When are we gonna deal with my anger issues?"

Recovery themes and the social adjustment rating scale bring to mind a recent participant for one last anger management vignette. A twenty-five-year-old male from Central America who was probation referred. Precipitant was in an altercation (pushing, shoving) at his family party. Everyone was slightly buzzed on alcohol and he felt that his brother had disrespected their mother. He confronted his brother, and a shoving match ensued. Latter felt afraid and called the police. One year probation and a referral to anger management.

As I've mentioned before, these groups have sporadic attendance. This is a fourteen-week program, and I am more flexible than probation concerning missed classes. I'd take into account work schedules, transportation, money, childcare, illness, relapses, etc. One woman drove five hours to group and five hours back home, weekly. Another had no car, no money, and no children. So she and her two young kids borrowed bikes and pedaled from the next city over. In the road along busy streets.

So my flexibility includes individual sessions if one participant shows up. My Central American client was sent to America following the murder of his father and attempt on his own life. (He lifted his shirt and showed me three bullet wound scars). His uncle is in the cartel and thought his dad ratted on him. His biggest stressor now is that his family is pressuring him to avenge his uncle. He feels his uncle will "finish the job."

CHAPTER TEN

Two Cents' Worth

I subscribe to Psychotherapy Networker, find it tremendously helpful, and would recommend it as regular reading for anyone in the field. But sometimes I want to throw it against the wall. Especially concerning specific case studies that I feel take a one-dimensional treatment approach with minimal systemic considerations. For example:

The March/April 2014 edition included "Whose therapy is it anyway? (When your client is uncommitted to change)," submitted by David Johnson, with a case commentary by Jay Efran and a response from Mr. Johnson.

The subject is a disheveled twenty-year-old Matthew who presents as resistant while listing multiple meds and diagnoses and having had twenty therapists. Also mentions that he is a victim of incest, has abandonment issues related to his mother, and has an alcoholic father. Mathew presents as hopeless and throws down the gauntlet of "give it your best shot, but it probably won't help!" Mathew makes some gains, disappears, and then resurfaces. The author's point here is that despite a clinician's treatment goals, you will only get as far as the client allows. This doesn't mean throwing in the towel. It means adjusting the goals to a more realistic vision of where the client is. Remember the title is "whose therapy," which suggests that if the clinician pushes the agenda, it's no longer the client's agenda.

A case commentary is then presented by Jay Efran. He congratulates David Johnson for "avoiding taking the bait and delving headlong into the juicier elements of Mathew's family story." Basically congratulates him for ignoring the systemic approach (Mathew's dad, alcoholic family elements). Or explaining the incest from a family perspective. This is a great self-fulfilling prophecy. Don't involve the family system, and when the client doesn't make progress, justify it by saying that this is not the clinician's agenda. This is great first-order change perspective. Is it any wonder that Matthew has had twenty therapists?

Back to Matthew—Jay Efran applauds the author for not being pushy (while comparing it to another therapist with a resistant adolescent female). I agree with that. He then questions the author's use of small talk by saying "I almost never open an initial session with small talk." I respect his style but question how rigid it sounds. Some clients absolutely need banal and nonthreatening conversation as an ice breaker. This allows them to relax, establish some normalcy, and develop trust. Others can't stand it, absolutely hate it. ("I'm not here to bullshit and pay you to talk about the weather.") In those cases, I respect their agenda and get right to it. So, however they want to precede, it's their agenda. I usually say, "So why did you call me?" And we move on. Or I ask, like Jay, what can I do for you?" Or "how did you get my name." I like "why did you call me?" Because it cuts right to the point. Jay adds that the partnership needs mutual goals to proceed. The author's response is that he and Jay have different "joining styles," and that Mathew would have seen through catch phrases that his previous twenty therapists had used to engage him.

My primary issue with this case study and subsequent commentary is that everything is first-order change oriented. Matthew is the identified patient over and over with twenty previous therapists and multiple meds. I wonder how many social workers, therapists, and psychiatrists had approached him on a linear, first-order manner. What role does this "obese, unkempt, unsanitary young man with a pimpled face" play within his family system? If he was sexually abused by his uncle and abandoned by his mother at age six, what role do these chronic PTSD and affective symptoms play within multiple systems?

Dad is an alleged alcoholic whom Matthew lives with. Is Matthew discouraged, in any way, from becoming more independent? Does he maintain the family homeostasis? Is he the primary caretaker for his alcoholic dad? Does Dad receive any treatment for his addiction? Is he in denial? Is he in recovery? Was any of this addiction family systems stuff addressed? I doubt it, because the theme of the article is two therapists reframing a resistant client so that the treatment is not about them.

How could Matthew be anything but pessimistic about therapy and meds? Which means most clinicians would look at years of treatment failure, slap that Axis II diagnosis on him, and maintain treatment homeostasis. I'm not a conspiracy type person, but if I was, I might think like this:

First-order treatment superficially addresses the issues while the second-order triggers remain unchanged. Homeostasis is maintained. Therapists see their clients, meds get prescribed, insurance claims are made, agencies get paid. Research is pharmaceutically driven, which reinforces short-term gains. And people like Matthew twist in the wind, become comfortable with self-fulfilling failure, have terrible self-esteem, remain stuck, and are labeled as difficult if they buck the system. It's good I'm not a conspiracy guy!

If I worked with Matthew, first of all, I would have seen him in his home. The initial treatment focus would be 1:1 with a mental health status, mood assessment, suicide assessment, substance abuse EVAL, and a history of any trauma or abuse. I would set short- and long-term goals. I would address hygiene, diet, exercise routines, and any healthy stress-reducing activities. An immediate topic would be what has helped (vs. what hasn't helped) in previous counseling experiences. Meds, therapists, styles, modalities, brief, long term, social service involvement, hospital stays. This elephant in the room would immediately have to be addressed. Twenty therapists, countless meds, continued symptoms, and (I think) a hopeless attitude.

I bet that I would meet Matthew's dad, probably in the first session. Maybe he would join us, be invited, or insist on being in the first session. Concern, intrusiveness, codependency, or maybe just the need to reinforce how fucked up his son is. Or to maybe deflect from his own addiction. I might hear double messages, like "I hope treatment works this time, but it never works!" or "Matthew could do better—but he can't change." I would remind Mathew that I include family work and would like his dad to join us at some point. As my relationship with Matthew strengthened, I would push harder for this. Unless Dad was a drunk or nuts, then the focus would immediately change with two identified patients. I would try to connect with everyone (including pets) in the home. Matthew just mentioned his dad. But in my experience, I sometimes meet family and friends who were never mentioned. ("Oh, this is my uncle; he lives in the attic.")

If Matthew began to make any progress (not missing sessions, having a brighter affect, and more motivation, better hygiene, increased activity level, weight loss), I would point out the potential ripple effects in the family system. I wouldn't bring up chaos theory and the butterfly effect, but I would reframe this as significant change (good or bad) creating anxiety and uneasiness. I would explain to anyone who would listen that Matthew's progress might upset the balance (homeostasis). I really believe this, so I explain the process to everyone. If Dad got involved, I'd attempt to engage him in some individual sessions. By giving his father some direct attention, this might reduce Matthew's caretaking. This would be huge, because many of my identified patient clients are deeply enmeshed in this codependent/caretaking role. Maybe his dad would address his alcohol use, which would be major second-order change (and create all kinds of butterfly effects).

Or maybe the second-order change scenario would be too disruptive to the family system. Maybe his dad would deny any addiction issues and stay hyper-focused on Matthew's multiple issues. I might get fired! Or Matthew might start progressing, the system would become unbalanced, and he would need to restore homeostasis by regressing. I would remind them that he was actually helping the family (but in a dysfunctional manner). I would normalize this as a sort of relapse, not a collapse. With a relapse, you stay proactive and keep moving forward. This is why the family piece of counseling is so crucial. My frustration comes from strictly individual approaches that just reinforce the identified patient role and first-order progress (sometimes).

Based on his treatment history, my approach with Matthew would be ego supportive, empowering every chance I got. Frequency and length of sessions would be up to him. As would be phone contact. I would explain how codependency runs in multiple directions. I would reframe and normalize as much as possible to offset the years of learned helplessness, codependency, and institutionalized thinking. If I got fired, I'd reframe it as the family system reacting to change. If they chose to resume counseling, they could call me any time. I would emphasize being rehired as a huge step to addressing difficult issues.

My other frustration comes from the lack of a holistic approach. I would give Matthew a free one-week pass to my gym. (My gym has been gracious enough to supply me with free passes.) There are often times such a lack of holistic techniques that this in itself would be second-order change. Or walking during our sessions. I'd do a nutritional and sleep hygiene eval. I'd explain hypoglycemia and mood effects, drinks rich in corn syrup and morbid obesity, weight loss and eating healthy (for life). I'd use examples from inpatient, outpatient, home-based, and foster care experiences. If Matthew developed trust for me, he might try some of the suggestions. If Matthew had a girlfriend, I know that I'd end up meeting her. Often, this leads to crisis related couples work. It's up to him. He's an adult and he makes the agenda. I would meet weekly, then twice per month, then monthly. I would encourage Matthew (and his dad or anyone else involved) to call for support. I find it very interesting that I give my clients my private number and they almost never abuse it. I remember working for an agency where this was not allowed. I think having access to my private number is reassuring. Knowing that they can call is calming during a crisis (so they don't have to call me).

In a nutshell, Matthew's life and counseling agenda and level of participation are his own. He's an adult who can do what he wants. I just think that as clinicians, we have to widen the menu of services and solutions offered.

And another thing...

Over the years, I've worked with a number of clients who would fall under the bipolar II diagnostic criteria. Hypo-manic episodes and dysthymia. No real manic craziness (usually). I was recently rereading the Bipolar II Disorder Workbook (New Harbinger Publications, Inc., 2013) and was intrigued by the "skills-based therapies for BPII" as described on page eighteen. These include cognitive behavioral therapy (CBT), dialectic behavior therapy (DBT), mindfulness-based cognitive therapy (MBCT), family-focused treatment (FFT), interpersonal and social rhythm therapy (IPSRT), and psychoeducation (PE).

Reading this left me of two minds. In some way, all these skill-based techniques are applicable to my bipolar II clients. The CBT applies due to their conditioned, negative thinking and how this translates into emotions and behaviors. Projective identification, self-fulfilling prophecies, negative feedback throughout their lives, being told that they're sick as well as double messages around effort and motivation. (Try harder, but you will most likely fail due to an inherent weakness.) If the thought process could be changed, so could the behavior. And vice versa, with positive behavior affecting negative thinking.

The DBT alters this by accepting the negativity (being in the here and now) and moving on in a proactive manner. (I have bipolar II disorder and need to address it and move on in my life.) Embracing treatment and a healthier lifestyle. Like CBT, DBT makes sense for the population I work with.

MBCT has aspects of both and emphasizes thoughts and feelings in the here and now. You then address these in a healthier manner. Like DBT, it means accepting the hand you have been dealt and moving on.

FFT addresses interpersonal and home stress by improving communication. Includes psychoeducation and problem solving. Hallelujah! Hallelujah! Had to say it twice. But as with all of them, I have issues which we will address later.

IPSRT focuses on resolving interpersonal issues, stabilizing routines, and managing symptoms. Yes, yes, and yes, and welcome to my anger management groups. It's common sense, and I bet that most therapists take this approach with their clients.

PE is a medical model approach that emphasizes the biological nature, med compliance, and psycho-social stressors. Where applicable, I use aspects of this with my clients.

All of these "skills-based therapies for bipolar II" lower depressive and manic episodes, decrease hospitalizations, enhance socialization skills, and, in some cases, decreases suicidal ideation. I consider them all helpful tools, and I use aspects of all six. Doesn't that make sense considering the diverse population I work with?

On the downside, each is way too simplistic for the clients I see. And once again, I can't help but think that the people I treat are not radically different from other therapists' clients. I guess this is the way I conceptualize pathology and mental illness. And because I see clients in their homes, I am immediately thrust into the midst of related individual, family, sibling, and couples' issues. It's a blended systemic soup which these six therapeutic approaches only partially address. For example:

There is no mention of substance abuse (addictive, recreational, abuse of prescription drugs, codependency). Good luck changing negative thinking in a chronically alcoholic family system. Or addressing med compliance when you are dealing with a poly drug abuser and a physician who over prescribes. And how about the change in family homeostasis? Or keeping the family in a dysfunctional homeostasis? Let's educate the family on how to treat their daughter's BPII symptoms without addressing the fact that Mom is significantly depressed, the brother is addicted to opiates, and Dad is abusive. First-order change with individual symptom management. Although IPSRT mentions "establishing and maintaining routines," where's the emphasis on diet, exercise, and sleep hygiene?

Let's look at my women's anger management group. Eight participants, with five diagnosed with bipolar II disorder. Several carry an ADD/ADHD diagnosis and complain that the stimulant meds exacerbate their mood swings. One clearly has PTSD symptoms, along with her bipolar symptoms. Her primary goal, as stated in the group, is to not be abusive when she becomes a mother. She was badly physically abused by her mother until she got old enough to defend herself. Then her dad took over domestic violence with a tag-team format. Still lives with her parents and avoids conflicts by remaining in her room. Her parents are in the process of being evicted, so she and her boyfriend are in the process of finding an apartment. Thank God! She has a significant learning disability that has impeded finding employment.

Two others with bipolar II are enmeshed in their family systems. They are repeatedly told that they are too impaired to be independent. Both of their mothers are disabled and need my clients' social securities to pay the rent. So they are caretakers in their family systems and have recreated this dynamic in their intimate relationships. Multi-generational codependency. The caretaking/identified patient dilemma! "I can't move out because my mother will be homeless!" The mothers sound severely mentally ill and receive minimal treatment. One of my younger members fought back as a child, was labelled as oppositional, and placed in "the system." She has been on meds ever since. Works, has a relationship, sounds like the healthiest member of her family system. Her confidence is seriously eroded from years of brainwashing. Any progress conflicts with her individual paradigm, with the result being cognitive dissonance. When I initially presented this to her, she got pissed off, defensive, and had to remind me how fucked up she was.

Most of these women in the anger management group have histories of trauma, domestic violence, and physical and sexual abuse. I think all have PTSD in some form. Their relationships suck, to put it frankly. They lack training, job skills, and all have financial issues. Most self-medicate or are in recovery. Oh yeah…and they're in anger management. So how do they fit in the "skills-based therapies for BPII"? They don't, really. Each of those approaches are valuable tools in combination. I know, I use them all. But taken separately, they miss 90 percent of what my clients are dealing with. Hence, my frustration with one-dimensional treatment approaches.

The DSM diagnostic criteria is another tool I use, but sometimes I feel like throwing it in my wood stove. It hardly applies to my clients and is one of the main reasons I've avoided insurance. For example, let's say I have a kid diagnosed with ADD/oppositional defiant disorder and I get invited to a school team meeting. The focus would be on managing him at school (understandable since we are at his school) while stabilizing his ADD issues with meds and a behavioral plan. Once again, very understandable from a symptom management, first-order perspective. Meanwhile, I'm sitting there thinking: *These teachers and adjustment counselors have no idea how much of a mess his family is.* Some idea, but not really.

The symptoms they see in school keep his family balanced in a dysfunctional manner.

The family doesn't trust the school or social services. They do trust me, so I am privy to all the zaniness.

This kid is repeating his scapegoat role in school while it has been molded and reinforced at home.

He is becoming his dad in the projective identification/self-fulfilling prophecy dance.

His family is blowing up, so his symptoms have exacerbated, so the school thinks he needs more counseling and meds.

His mom heeds the school's advice, and he goes back to his doctor, who increases his meds.

Parents blame the school; school blames the parents. Then they ask me why counseling isn't working.

I'm limited in what I can say due to confidentiality, a fear of losing the family's trust, and a realization that most of them have no idea of what I'm talking about.

And you wonder why people often say "counseling doesn't work…meds don't work…what he really needs is a smack on the ass."

I realize that this chapter has kind of been all over the place: a critique of a case study, bipolar II treatment paradigms and in oppositional child in a school setting. Systemic work is usually all over the place with new material popping up. It's that Gesalt thing!

CHAPTER ELEVEN

Home-Based Bereavement Counseling

I once worked with a family whom I had known from 1:1 counseling with their dad and couples counseling with both parents. Approximately two years after termination, Dad was killed in an automobile accident. His widow called for bereavement counseling for the entire family (three children, along with herself). They were numbed by the sudden loss. This was emotional for me because of my working relationship with both parents. This was also the first family for whom I provided home-based grief counseling. Prior to this, I had worked with a family whose daughter's best friend had been brutally murdered. But this was a friend, not an immediate member of the family whom I had known.

So when I arrived for the initial meeting, everyone was in shock. We met in the living room, where I was surrounded by family pictures. I began by asking about the story behind each picture. Everywhere were happy family memories contrasted with disbelief and sadness. The nine-year-old daughter immediately pulled out a family photo album, and this became the focus of all our subsequent sessions. Each week, different pictures were highlighted, followed by memorabilia and personal items. All I did was facilitate the conversation around the objects handed to me. This eventually morphed into individual counseling for the nine-year-old who had been the closest to her dad and was the most distressed.

Somehow this case got passed through the grapevine, and I began to get bereavement referrals. One young mom who had just lost her husband to cancer called and said she was given my name because I specialized in grief counseling. I said that I specialized in home-based counseling, and that sometimes included bereavement therapy. This was another classic example of something I never really studied in school (or specialized in) being the referring precipitant. Clients and therapists kept sending me similar cases. I would just do my Gestalt/family systems/ego supportive thing. Like interventions or angry adolescent girls or chaotic family systems. Actually, I would say the last one is my specialty.

So my new client presented as a young widow in shock, with two young and traumatized sons. The older was twelve, angry, and struggling to focus in school. His life had just been turned upside down. We alternated individual and family sessions that included parenting consultations. Mom had her own individual therapist.

This counseling happened in stages. Stage one was strictly grief work, with an emphasis on sadness, anger, loss, shock, abrupt changes in the family system, normalizing through familiar routines, and reframing moodiness and oppositional behavior. This was an athletic family, and both 1:1 and sibling meetings always involved sports. Whiffle ball in the back yard, catch with a football, and hockey in the cellar. The latter could be very physical, with the twelve-year-old unable to tolerate losing or performing poorly. Probably displacing his anger on competitive sports. His "winning means everything" attitude diminished as counseling progressed.

Therapy with mom was about her kids' progress and the incredibly sad fact that she was a young widow with two sons. I quickly realized that I was a transitional figure for this family, especially since treatment was home based. A male figure for Mom to share personal issues and a surrogate father figure for the angry boys to literally bounce plastic pucks off of. This is why I believe that countertransference and boundaries are so crucial, especially in home-based work.

The second stage happened at about six months. Both boys were convinced that their mother would never date or remarry. Prior to this, the focus was on loss and maintaining. Now Mom realized that she was young and didn't want to raise her boys alone. She met someone, and this generated all kinds of questions.

"How do I tell the boys?"

"When should he meet the boys?"

"How much contact should they have?"

"How much time should I spend with him?"

One of her fears was that if it didn't work out, her boys would experience another loss. Initially, both were pissed and wanted nothing to do with Joe. This began to shift when he became familiar with both boys and became "Mom's boyfriend." Joe being accepted actually exacerbated Mom's fears of the impact if the relationship didn't work out. This process took a little over a year.

Joe was a good guy who played sports with the boys and endeared himself to the family. But he wasn't prepared to assume a stepfather's role, so the relationship ended. This was stage three of the bereavement counseling. A new loss that echoed the most painful family loss. The older boy, now an adolescent, was sad and angry. This naturally brought up memories of his dad's death. My role was to separate the two losses. The first was his dad, the first or second most important figure in his life. The second was mom's boyfriend, the first intimate relationship since Dad had passed. A good guy who they all had fun with. Whether due to a higher level of maturity, experience with loss, rebounding, counseling, or whatever, the family moved fairly quickly through this process. Mom realized that she needed to move on and that her kids were going to be okay. The latter realization was huge.

This was one of those families I saw sporadically but on a consistent basis. Weekly, every other week, monthly, every few months, then as needed, and then finishing up. When it became every few months, my primary focus was reinforcing what a great single parent she was. Both boys were doing well. Mom began dating a guy whom her sons loved. Two years later, I bumped into mom who proudly showed me her engagement ring. Two years later, I bumped into her again and she introduced me to her husband and new baby daughter. Said that both her sons were doing well. When I think back to that case, I firmly believe that the outreach format allowed me to navigate through stages of grief and family development.

Another family that was referred to me was grieving over the cancer-related death of the mother. They were stunned by the loss in what sounded like a matriarchal family system. Widowed dad and two adolescents (son and daughter). Mom had passed approximately one year prior to my involvement. She had been the CEO of a company, very smart, and the primary breadwinner. I worked with this family for three and a half years. Family meetings with all three, individual with dad (Dave), and occasional individual with Anne (19) and Cory (15).

Dave initially contacted me and said that he had lost his wife after a twenty-year marriage. All three presented as significantly depressed, with Dave concerned that he was overbearing with his kids. He was also morbidly obese. Actually, he was the opposite of overbearing. He was passive, probably due to his personality and affective symptoms. He admitted that along with being responsible for a large part of the family income, his late wife was also the limit setter.

Anne mirrored her mother's drive and high functioning behavior. Straight A's and musical talents with college scholarships awaiting. I immediately saw that she was parentified with both Cory and her dad. Made sense: she was taking Mom's place. She was more animated and engaged in the therapy process. Cory was more like his dad: quiet, reserved, and passive. He was also resentful of his sister "trying to be like my mother"; this was a no-win scenario for everyone but especially Anne. The more she tried to organize the family, the more resentful Cory became.

Cory was also in that weird "second banana" sibling position where he could never measure up to his big sister. She still is one of the brightest and most talented kids I've ever worked with. Cory's lack of accomplishments, such as so-so grades, were magnified by Anne's successes. I knew right away that the bereavement therapy would include empowering Dad as a single parent, reducing Anne's parentified role, and removing Cory from the identified patient role. His role was further solidified by his angry/aggressive play themes and personal interests. He was slightly obsessed with soldiers and guns and violent video games. Liked to dress in fatigues. He also had zero interest in displacing these feelings in competitive school sports or any physical type outlet. He had minimal interest in school, presented with socialization issues (according to Dave), fought with his sister, and had what seemed to be the prerequisite ADD/ADHD diagnosis. He was on stimulant meds, as were most of the boys who were referred to me. I saw him as depressed, grieving, and with some Asperger characteristics. He also reflected his dad's temperament and disposition.

Since Cory was already in the identified patient role, we began alternating family session and individual sessions. He wasn't crazy about meeting 1:1 but was punctual and respectful. Initially, he resisted discussing his mom's death because it triggered him and made him appropriately sad. I was concerned about his vegetative symptoms and referred him to a nurse practitioner, who included his dad in psychopharm meetings. This was the one person who was always cautious with meds, especially with kids. She decided against prescribing anything and referred them back to me. She saw them several times and encouraged the bereavement work. Anne was now in college, with the family sessions addressing Dad's loneliness, lifestyle, and relationship with Cory.

Cory continued to be obsessed with guns, knives, soldiers, and warfare. It was cathartic, but obviously worrisome. This was several years after the Columbine murders, so need I say more? He wasn't mean spirited and showed no symptoms of a budding sociopathy. Still made me nervous, and these aggressive themes were repeatedly brought up in individual and family meetings. This was also a male thing, wanting to shoot guns and have a career in the military. Dave supported his interest in guns. Gave him a bb gun, then a twenty-two when he was older, and, finally, a shotgun. I would have preferred he play chess and be on the football team, but it wasn't my call. I would arrive for a session and Cory would show me his guns, bullets, and knife collection. He would painstakingly explain the safety features and show me how he kept his guns and ammo separate and always locked up. He became a member of the NRA, joined a gun club, and began skeet shooting competition.

My main dilemma was separating my personal beliefs and countertransference from the clinical picture. It was one of those bizarro world times when I'd catch myself thinking: *If you had told me that I'd be sitting on the edge of my client's bed, holding a shotgun and examining ammo with my client, a young, depressed, and withdrawn male, following a series of school shootings by young, depressed males while encouraging his NRA involvement and proficiency at skeet shooting.* The thing is, he was being responsible, and his Dad was pleased by his interest and motivation. Plus, his dad supported his hobbies, whether I approved or not. At least I could assess his mood and functioning on an ongoing basis. Strange stuff, this outreach counseling! I felt that the timing and weirdness of this case were fascinating, so I submitted a case study to a counseling journal. It was promptly rejected. I think I scared them.

Cory and I talked a lot about hunting. I was honest, saying that I supported hunting for food. As an omnivore, I had no right criticizing people who didn't just buy meat neatly wrapped. I also disclosed that as a teenager living in the woods, I had a .22. Myself and several friends would "hunt" for fun, shooting birds, woodchucks, and squirrels. Never for food, so we were basically murdering innocent animals. Worst thing I ever did, and I regretted the selfishness and succumbing to peer pressure as an adolescent. Cory was stunned by my honesty and emotional response. Talk about countertransference!

But there was a lot going on here. This was about respect for life, dangerous weapons, grieving, mood disorders, personal responsibility, peer pressure, repressing emotions as a male, school shootings, all layered with my own baggage. One day, I arrived for our session and Cory was sitting with a buddy in his hot tub, shooting pellet pistols. As I approached, one of them nailed a bird, and I saw it fall to the ground. First, Cory denied it, then said it was an accident, then said that he only wounded it. I said that if that was the case, he had an injured animal to tend to. Then he begged me not to tell his dad. I agreed if he promised not to murder any more animals. I reminded him of this agreement for the remainder of our counseling experience.

We had ongoing discussions about the right to bear arms and gun control. He generally agreed with my position, that it is a constitutional right to have weapons, that unstable people violate this right, that hunters don't need assault rifles, and that background checks make sense. He became very accomplished at skeet shooting, the first ego-supportive outlet he had since we'd began working together. He was definitely better at that than his sister! His accomplishments were noted by his family, which was new to the family system. Usually, Anne received all the accolades. Interestingly, she took up the bow and arrow and began to accompany Cory and Dave to the gun club. (Anything you can do...) They asked me to accompany them to the gun club, and I said I couldn't due to boundaries. They asked me to have supper with them, and I said, again, it was a boundary issue. I usually settled for a glass of water.

Sitting with them while they ate was diagnostic due to their obesity issues and terrible diet. Mom used to cook healthy meals. Now Dave would return home exhausted and depressed with little energy to cook. Fast food was quicker and more convenient. With the grief counseling having progressed and Cory more animated and motivated, my focus turned to their unhealthy diets. Was this full circle or what? I get hired to provide bereavement counseling to a sad and depressed family, and the psychotherapy morphs into at-risk disordered eating. Actually, it's another example of the butterfly effect.

Cory asked his dad to fire me so that I could socialize with the family. A tremendous compliment but I, again, reinforced my boundaries. Once a client, always a client! I did attend a music recital for Anne at the request of all three. I emphasized that this was an exception while reinforcing that my role was family therapist. Dave was lonely with socialization issues, so we addressed his need to not isolate.

As is almost always the case, the 1:1s with Cory were relaxed, always ego supportive, and minimally confrontational. The family meetings were more serious and anxiety provoking, due to his dad and Anne being present. The subject matter was also more intense: Mom's illness and death, Dave beginning to date, chores, school performance, and sibling issues. I met Anne's new boyfriend, who sat in on some family meetings, and, you guessed it, a couples meeting or two at Anne's request. He was (surprise) more like Dave: laid back and less driven. Anne remained the dynamo in school and then her career. Just like her mother. I wondered about the "which came first...chicken or the egg" thing! Was it genetic...Mom's personality in the genes...or system, Anne being subtly groomed and expected to be the next matriarch? Probably both.

I pointed out that we had a shared experience. When I was twenty, my mother had died of lung cancer. I described my reaction and the process of grief. They were inquisitive but supportive and respectful.

Cory's school performance remained average, and it was evident that academics was not his thing. He remained fascinated with guns, and I complimented his being both cautious and responsible. He was animated, more verbal, with no apparent vegetative symptoms. I, again, thought about guns, depressed young males, and Columbine. I was struck by what I never learned in graduate school but had experienced in home-based counseling. Let's see... How about seeing clients in their homes, prevention work, group dynamics (maybe a little bit), addiction (very little), adolescent counseling (somewhat), systems work (one course), holistic techniques (nada), anger management (not at all), trauma (very little), eating disorders (only a mouthful), PTSD (say what?), crazy couples, multi-problem scenarios? I learned all of this on the fly. And for several years, I was attending graduate school while working in inpatient psychiatry. So I was applying what I learned in my job to my graduate studies, not vice versa. A lot of the graduate students had zero clinical experience and no idea what I was talking about.

But back to Cory and home-based grief counseling. If I had met the family two and a half years earlier, the thought of him having guns might have sent me packing. The countertransference was substantial: mother's death from cancer, guns, and killing animals. My supervision/consultation group helped me step back and look at the clinical picture. They were experienced clinicians. I think the less experienced therapists in previous (agency) supervision groups would have freaked out. Which would have raised my anxiety and question my choices. Agency and personal liability issues!

Anne was now in college and living away from home. When she was home, she requested individual sessions. When available, she participated in family therapy. Being in school literally removed her from her parentified role with Dave and Cory. This was significant second-order change and a primary topic in the family sessions. She had to let go of this role, and it wasn't easy. Individual sessions with Dave revolved around his parenting (with Anne less involved), dating, his diet and weight issues. Cory had matured with better grades and brighter affect. He also began to develop interests that did not include themes of violence. My 1:1 sessions with him addressed developmental issues: adolescent sexuality, peer relationships, school, issues with his sister's boyfriend, and his dad dating. We also discussed how his family had grown since his mom's death.

My work with Cory's family lasted three and a half years. We went from weekly to twice a month to monthly to as needed, and then terminated services. Looking back, I would call this systemic bereavement counseling with two identified patients: Dave and Cory. Both were significantly depressed. Dave's symptoms reinforced Anne's parentification. She displayed her grief differently and was too busy to have the same vegetative symptoms. She was just like Mom, while Cory was just like Dad. As adolescents often do, Cory acted out his depression, which served to reinforce his scapegoat role, make Dave feel more inadequate as a struggling single parent, and reinforced Anne's need to take control. I explained all of this to them, and they absolutely got it. The major sibling issue was both Anne and Cory playing out their family roles.

Technically, this was grief counseling (individual and family) with holistic aspects (diet, exercise). For me, it's always ego supportive and systemic. I constantly had to be aware of my countertransference and boundaries. I had to be aware of peripheral issues (school shootings by depressed young males) while retaining my objectivity. Systems work is complicated and long term. This was three and a half years of developmental family issues. Getting over a significant loss, Dad dating, Anne going to college, adolescent peer and self-esteem issues. With evolving behavior: knives and combat fatigues, joining the NRA, and accomplished skeet shooting. We all had to trust the process.

When I reread this chapter, I realized how all three cases began with grief and loss and then morphed into developmental and personal longer term issues. And these issues were exacerbated by the original precipitant. I think some type of loss is woven into most counseling. Loss of youth, health, work, loved ones, relationships, and pets. The stages of grief bounce back and forth. I think about that fifteen-year-old girl who grieved her mother's AIDS-related impending death. Only to have her mother recover!

Home-Based Counseling with Axis II Clients

Axis II is a diagnostic category from the *Diagnostic and Statistical Manual of Mental Disorders, Fourth Edition.* Also called personality disorders (borderline, paranoid, narcissistic, obsessive compulsive, etc.). I like the definition, John Ingram Walken provided in *Complete Mental Health* (2010):

> A pervasive pattern of behavior that remarkably deviates from cultural expectations and leads to impairment in work, love and friendships characterized by constant blaming, excuse making and refusal to take responsibility for personal behavior... begins in adolescence or early adulthood and is unrelated to drug abuse, a medical condition, or in other mental disorder (page 149).

I included the whole definition because of its accuracy. These are the most challenging cases I have in home-based work as well as anger management and prevention groups. Usually, they are exacerbated by substance abuse or depression.

This isn't news to anyone with clinical experience. What I see is a perfect storm of pathology: classic symptoms of conduct disorder, antisocial behavior, narcissistic, borderline, and dependent personality features. Along with paranoia and psychotic symptoms in extreme cases. Intensified developmental factors, especially if the identified client is an adolescent. And the almost always present systemic features. Like I said, the perfect storm!

The systemic aspect has a long-term double message. The surface message, "my kid is screwed up," highlights the behavioral (oppositional, bullying, risk taking) and affective (depression, sadness, self-destructive). Little or no attention is paid to the systemic factors: parenting couple, active addiction within the immediate family, loss, domestic violence, trauma, as well as long term physical and mental issues within the family. So the secondary or unspoken message is "My kid's symptoms are behavioral, voluntary, basically under his control." Therefore, not indicating any real pathology. Screwed up...but not that screwed up! This makes perfect sense because nobody wants to think that their child is seriously disturbed. In my experience, most of the time they are not. It's usually developmental or situational. But every once in a while, I meet an adolescent or young adult who has consistently refused treatment or has not responded to previous professional help. The family has heard about my home-based approach, which makes sense due to their child refusing to go to a clinic (or even get in the car). If the situation is primarily developmental, treatment can often be short term, involving couples consults, self-esteem emphasis, and a lot of reframing and normalizing. Parents begin to work better as a team while the dependency/autonomy teen issues become viewed as an irritating part of growing up. The mood changes, attitudes get adjusted, and you can feel a genuine sigh of relief from everyone.

But in rare cases, I'm told that the son has always bullied his sibs, turns everything around, and never takes responsibility for his own actions. Ever! I always question whether this is just another example of scapegoating, with projective identification and the dreaded self-fulfilling prophecy, and then I talk to their son or daughter. The child takes no responsibility for his or her actions, blames everyone else, and refuses help because it's everyone else's fault. Says the same thing to teachers, guidance counselors, social workers... Everybody! And they feel genuine outrage that they are being put in this position. Usually with a very pronounced narcissistic slant. Ah, this isn't good.

The parents look at me with this spooked deer-in-the-headlights expression. Do something...please. But don't say that our kid is as fucked up as we fear. So they stay angry (and often powerless) with his behavior. If the couple are at odds, one usually scapegoats and the other defends and enables. Very black and white, which reinforces the pathology.

The double message is extreme. On the surface, he is told "You're bad!" which is reinforced by both but especially the enabler. The unspoken secondary message is to maintain the homeostasis. "You have all the control and power within the family system." So, you end up with an acting-out, identified patient within a depressed family system.

One such referral was a fourteen-year-old boy "possibly depressed" and missing a lot of school. In actuality, he was paranoid, fairly psychotic, and abusive to his younger sister. The family had some money, so DSS and the police were circumvented. By the time I saw the family, the boy didn't attend school at all. When I expressed my concerns, both parents argued that it wasn't that bad. Yes, it was that bad! He was referred for a med eval and saw a therapist (I hope) through the same agency.

Another referral involved a sixteen-year-old female in high school. Obviously paranoid, or at least hypervigilant. Acted this way with her family. Both her parents and sibs had been walking on eggshells for years. She supposedly had no history of physical abuse, sexual abuse, or major trauma, but she couldn't sit in a room alone with me. The parents tried but eventually gave in and enabled her. Some type of paranoid personality disorder. When she finally agreed to some shortened 1:1 sessions, with family in an adjoining room, she never relaxed! This was clearly diagnostic, because I establish trust with my clients fast. Even the ones who need a testing period trust me to proceed with that testing period, like Erica and her need to have control over our sessions. This was a totally different situation.

This case also brought up a dilemma for me. As you've figured out by now, I'm a systems guy who tries very hard to remove the identified patient from their reinforced pathological role. By education, reframing, normalizing, identifying systemic stressors, reinforcing age-appropriate behavior, and enhancing self-esteem. Also, by seeing clients in their primary systems (immediate and extended family), I am privy to double messages, untreated family members, parentified status, and general systemic dysfunction. As a result, I have a different slant on Axis II disorders. I can't say with absolute certainty whether the Axis II referrals are hardwired to present as such or products of their environment. Is it the chicken or the egg? Is the behavior singled out, labelled, and reinforced by the family and multiple systems? Or does conduct disordered behavior begin at a young age and the family basically gives in to avoid problems? I had an adult male referred to me for individual counseling. All the classic themes of a sociopathic personality disorder. Recently paroled for an armed robbery. Opiate addiction history. No remorse for his actions and minimal empathy for anyone. He would periodically leave his wife and kids because the former was "being a bitch." He would move into his parents' lavish downstairs apartment and bring women home. One time I went to see him at this apartment and his mother was bringing him dinner (literally) on a silver platter. He would stay for a while and then return to his family because his wife "isn't being a bitch anymore."

So was this guy born with a predisposition for sociopathy with early conduct disordered warning signs? Or did his culture, ethnicity, parental experiences, gender expectations, and entitlement (exacerbated by criminal behavior, deviant peer relationships, and addiction) create what I saw? I think it's both, but I clearly do not want to reinforce the systemic piece. I also do not want to minimize the behavior and become another enabling figure. So what I did with this guy was focus on symptoms and healthy behavior. Recognizing depression and anxiety, minimizing any substance use, encouraging a commitment to both individual and couples counseling. Basically reinforce healthy behavior as a father and husband. Hopefully, any positive behavior would minimize the scapegoating and enabling within his family. He wanted separation (new job) from his family but was discouraged at every attempt. Regardless of his diagnosis, that homeostasis thing was alive and well within his family system. With the projective identification. His mother knew that he saw me for 1:1 counseling, but his dad was not told. The latter "didn't believe" in counseling and felt his son couldn't change. A very enmeshed family with a lot of double messages.

If these referrals display a thought disorder or debilitating paranoia, I often suggest a med evaluation. This is often met with resistance, especially with an adolescent. "Our kid is so screwed up she needs meds!" Even if the identified patient is scapegoated, there is often denial about the extent of the problem. When I meet a new client or family, I'm very clear about my position on meds. Unless the person's level of functioning is dramatically compromised, I would prefer talk therapy with behavioral and holistic techniques. I do not want people to prioritize drugs over a healthy lifestyle. Identify stressors and begin to learn healthier lifelong coping mechanisms. Begin to address second-order issues in a healthier environment. Whether it's deserved or not, the referred client is usually stuck within that identified patient role. Meds can remove them or firmly entrench them in that role. "My daughter is on medication, so she's really messed up!"

Some referrals require immediate crisis assessments for inpatient and meds. One time I was referred a fifteen-year-old-boy who had missed school for approximately one month. His situation was mentioned as an aside while I was consulting with a school psychologist in regard to another case. Nobody had seen this kid for a while, and since I did outreach, I called his mother and made an appointment after having introduced myself. I went to his house the next day. Probably the most depressed individual I've ever met, aside from hospitalized patients. I remember his crying! I asked him how he was, and a steady stream of tears began to pour out of each eye. Literally formed a puddle on the floor. (I remember staring at the extent of the puddle at the end of our session). On a suicidal scale of one to ten, he was about an eight. Ruminating thoughts of dying from when he opened his eyes in the morning. Over the past week, a well thought-out plan on where and how to hang himself. Several months before, a close friend had committed suicide. This friend took his own life on the one-year anniversary of a mutual friend having taken his life. So this kid was grieving two deaths, one very recent, and was exhibiting severe vegetative symptoms including no motivation, a sleep and appetite disturbance, blank affect, and psychomotor retardation. And on the suicidal ideation continuum, he was way down the end. An adolescent. Two close deaths from suicide. I mean, this was textbook stuff.

I immediately told him that I was afraid for his safety and that his mom had to be involved in the conversation. I advised his mother to take him to the emergency room. She was surprised but did as I suggested. In a follow up call to his house, his mother said that he had been assessed, referred to an outpatient therapist, and sent home. I guess they didn't see him as much at risk as I did. I think that this was a financial decision, based on insurance coverage. If this had happened twenty years ago, I'd bet my house that he would have been hospitalized. Times have changed. Liability versus managed care. What I think about is how I just stumbled upon a very distraught kid.

I realize that I have veered off the Axis II path and onto the Axis I diagnostic route. I would have diagnosed him with a major depression and PTSD. I only knew him for one and a half hours. No Axis II symptoms reported or viewed through a narrow time frame. But this does bring up interesting diagnostic questions.

This is when it gets tricky and I badly need the objectivity of consultation. Clinicians are reluctant to use an Axis II diagnosis for teens for two main reasons. The most important is brain development. An adolescent brain is not the finished product. The other reason is the implication of being labeled with such a severe diagnosis. For me, add the systemic features, the chicken or the egg dynamic.

I've seen latency-aged (ten to twelve) kids that display classic personality disordered symptoms (taking no responsibility, blaming, showing no empathy) but some of that is classic latency/teen behavior. I don't want to pressure dysfunctional family homeostasis by reinforcing his identified patient role. I also do not want to minimize severe personality symptoms and enable developing pathology. When an Axis II presents himself or herself in counseling, the systemic features almost always play into maintaining homeostasis.

I've previously mentioned that my referrals have come with repetitive themes and presenting problems. This happened with bereavement, HIV, foster family therapy, and anger management. More specifically, very pissed off adolescent girls, oppositional/defiant teenaged boys. The main drawing card has always been multi problem families in a home-based format. And always substance abuse and addiction.

The Blind Leading the Blind:
Providing Counseling Services to Other Therapists and their Families

I have also been providing counseling services to other clinicians, significant others, and children for about fifteen years. It began with individual therapists referring their clients for in-home family treatment. Or referring an adult or child for 1:1, and with the referring therapist already providing family or system couples work.

Or the referral would be a short-term anger management or substance abuse evaluation. These same clinicians began to hire me to provide home-based services for their own families or adolescents. The reasons were threefold. First, they felt that home-based services provided more confidentiality. They were worried that a therapist seeking counseling services would negatively impact their reputation. Secondly, they heard positive things (usually) from the individuals and families they referred to me. And lastly, they were intrigued by the idea of outreach counseling. They've never experienced it, but they see the potential benefits.

At the beginning, working with other therapists was all about my own self-esteem, which affected my countertransference. This involved my education level: masters. I was working with PhDs and MDs; plus, I wasn't licensed. I'd never had kids, but I was providing parental advice. I was single and providing paid advice to couples in distress. I was providing family therapy to family therapists, individual counseling to 1:1 therapists. And substance abuse counseling to substance abuse professionals. Some were recovered addicts or alcoholics. I was never an addict or alcoholic. I also wondered how they would relate to my systemic approach. Would they resist like everybody else (initially) did? Would I back off because I was intimidated by their credentials? Would they be close-minded and stuck in their own orientation? Would I get fired quicker and develop a terrible reputation? Would they stop sending me referrals? I also wondered about the pathology I'd be dealing with. In the back of my mind was a statement made years ago by another therapist: that some therapists might be severely impaired.

Well, I've found the opposite to be true. Bright and motivated and well-educated people who trust me to do my systemic/Gestalt/mixed treatment modality thing. And with an open mind. They have blind spots, usually around identified patients and family homeostasis. Similar to non-clinical people, but open to my interpretations. Some bipolar II, substance misuse, narcissism, PTSD, relationship and family issues. Some are clearly parentified within their family systems (hence the reason for becoming therapists). I've seen most in their homes, but I also go to their offices. Sit in their waiting room. It's kinda refreshing since all my work is outreach. We joke about who should sit in which chair. It's very comfortable, and confidentiality is maintained.

I'm obviously there to see the therapist!

Working with clinicians and their families definitely has some unique features. The adults are hyperalert for warning signs they experience every day in their practices. Affective and substance-related warning signs: changes in mood, poorer grades, loss of interest and motivation, and a change in oppositional/defiant behavior that appears more than developmental. They see me as an objective set of eyes when they know they can't be totally objective. On an intellectual level, they know what's going on. Their kids can be manipulative because they know that their parents know, or at least think they know. Like the parent who contacted me because her artistic adolescent son was drawing primarily in black, with themes of doom. Was he suicidal or homicidal? Actually, he was defiant and knew he'd get a rise out of his mother if he used black ink. Maybe she would back off the curfew if she was worried about him. He admitted this. Pretty slick!

Some daughters have become pseudo shrinks for their friends. They've had empathy and communication skills and prevention education role modeled for them their whole lives. Makes sense that they would share this with needy friends. How many have said "I'm the one they come and talk to about boys, sex, drugs, and cutting?" And they always add that they just can't understand why. Well, I know why. I remind them that they are twelve years old, in the seventh grade, not ready for a professional counseling life. Actually, it could be viewed as an initial stage of codependency, and I wonder how the info I provide might exacerbate this process. I emphasize that their empathy can be a trap.

Sometimes the adults are embarrassed that they have to hire another professional to provide basically the same services that they provide. It really is about an objective set of eyes looking at systemic nuances. Or high functioning individuals and couples addressing multiple stressors. Sometimes I think they have more on their plates because their clinical background allows them to have more on their plates. A catch twenty-two. Working with psycopharmacoligists always brings up my countertransference. Who am I to suggest meds with a med expert? I deal with my self-doubt and move on. What helps is the holistic approach. Professionals are usually open to diet, exercise, sleep hygiene, and breathing exercises.

All the clinicians I have worked with deal with managed care and insurance limitations. They like the flexibility that home-based systems work provides.

Usually one parent is in the mental health field, and the other is not. I try not to be too chummy (which is easy to do) with the other clinician, which could make the other parent feel less knowledgeable or less directly involved. I also have to be aware of my own boundaries. I always have questions, either directly or indirectly, related to the case, especially with medical doctors. But they're not paying me to answer questions that have nothing to do with why they hired me. The thing is, they know a lot more about meds and medical procedures. I usually limit questions to one at the end of our session.

Sometimes we share clients, which has taken me some getting used to. Consulting with a clinician about a case we share while I'm professionally involved with that clinician or her family. This was awkward at first, but I've developed a comfort level. I may see a therapist 1:1 and spend ten additional minutes discussing the progress of the family that therapist referred to me. I continued to get referrals from professionals, whom I regard very highly for their work, but this is somewhat of a conflict of interest. As a result, I refer clients to the agencies of the clinicians I work with. Otherwise, my subjectivity from having the therapist as a client might affect my reasons for referral. If this sounds slightly convoluted and hypocritical, well, I guess it is. But it appears to be effective.

I've worked with some clinicians and their families whom I've liked a lot and would enjoy socializing with if they were not my clients. Many are smarter, and some are clearly higher functioning than me. But once a client, always a client. Many of the referrals are long- term clients being referred for a specific piece of work. Short-term anger management, a substance abuse assessment, brief couples work. Many refer me their kids for an at-risk evaluation. This is really prevention work with the kids (usually) in good shape.

CONCLUSION

Writing this book has clarified and reinforced concepts and themes related to my counseling experiences. The first thing is trust. From my clients, supervisors, and other clinicians. The trust of executive directors to allow me to work as independently as possible within an agency's framework. Trusting me to be able to negotiate the complications of working with a twelve-year-old girl (and her younger female sibs) while their mother was pursuing a lawsuit against her former male therapist for sexual misconduct. Also, Mom's trust that I wasn't like her former therapist.

This gave me confidence to follow my instincts and think outside the box. My AIDS awareness program was a great example of this. That agency went through multiple turnovers regarding the directors. The one common theme was positive feedback and encouragement to keep developing the program. And they were all understanding about how difficult it was for me to document progress. AIDS awareness took off in all sorts of directions because individual staff trusted the concept and wanted to expand the services.

So when I went into private practice, nothing really changed except for a decrease in paperwork and bureaucracy. As I've mentioned throughout this book, effective treatment was based on facilitating relationships. Clients, their families, staff, neighbors, dogs! No relationships meant no effective treatment!

And these relationships were crucial because of my core belief in second-order change. I stir up a lot of shit that wouldn't be addressed if I just focused on the presenting problem. Remember that foster care agency that freaked out when I started talking about the dynamics of foster family therapy? They didn't want to know about aspects of dysfunction built into the system. Systemic homeostasis gets shaken up, and it shouldn't be immediately restored. That's the whole point! My clients have usually trusted me enough to work with the upheaval. And the referring therapists don't panic. They usually just say, "Let him do his thing."

This trust has changed my referral process for the past ten years. No more advertising or marketing. I give out business cards, but that's it. All my referrals come from clients, former clients, and other professionals. I used to explain (almost defensively) how I provided counseling differently. Outreach, mixed modalities, experiential, no insurance. Some clients were apprehensive, especially if they had medical insurance. Now, when I start to explain my approach, it usually goes like this: They say, "You don't accept insurance, and you see all your clients in their homes. I like that! You like to involve the whole family and do parenting consults. I like that. Can we make an appointment?" Every once in a while, I'll get someone who wants my credentials or a rationale for why I do outreach. But for the most part, they have been prepared by their own therapist, whom they trust.

This is where it gets interesting. It's that second-order change thing. Change—a new paradigm. If currently involved in individual therapy, this is first order presented with one side is given. The therapist has an obvious bias because this is their client. So the consensus is (1) involve the spouse or children, and (2) home-based gives me a more accurate view. But that means objectively looking at the part you play in the situation. There is usually pushback, and then it's up to my countertransference. I've been abruptly and angrily fired, then rehired. I've been fired while getting positive feedback on my work. Once I was given a tip for the terminating session. A defensive parent who denied any addiction. But my work was too threatening to the family homeostasis. I got it and thanked everyone for their hard work. Maybe a seed was planted and things would change in the future.

Discussing common interests is a tremendous joining mechanism, plus those common interests reduce anxiety during periods of intense work. Since I'm in my client's home, I'm surrounded by familiar and comforting items. With kids, it's toys. Tours are part of the joining process. And if we have something in common, this is where the relationship really begins. Music, movies, pets, current news, history, the cosmos, evolution... It just goes on and on! Specifically, The Beatles, dinosaurs, Bruce Lee, Godzilla, *The Walking Dead*, sports, and food, which is huge. For example:

An angry and resistant sixteen-year-old shows me his bedroom at his mother's request. He has several Beatles posters which I comment on; and he opens up a chest and pulls out imported Beatles albums that I have never seen. I think he noticed the goosebumps!

After an explosive couple's session, I bump into their fourteen-year-old daughter and a friend. They proudly inform me that they are listening to *Sgt. Pepper* on vinyl. They ask if I like The Beatles. Oh yeah!

My rapid cycling bipolar II client calls me in crisis. She's been scanning the hemlock society site (again) so we make a safety contract. Stay off that goddamn site! And listen to Rubber Soul. Beatles music therapy!

One major regret was never developing my foster family therapy format into an ongoing program. The issue was that I wanted to work independently and not accept third-party payments, and the foster families could not self-pay. They had multiple kids and needed to use their available insurance. The other complication was the resistance to looking at foster families from a family systems point of view. Remember that pissed-off foster care agency? I've mentioned the support I received from foster parents, clients, social workers, and other clinicians. People directly involved wanted the service developed. People indirectly involved couldn't relate! Very sad.

I should mention here that those three clinical vignettes occurred within the same month. And that, at the end of that month, I had my annual Beatles festival at my house. Karma? It makes sense to me because I've always considered the Beatles phenomenon as quasi-religious experience; you tell me!

This was twenty years ago, and as I've already mentioned, the logistics made it more difficult maybe impossible. A home-based approach with a systemic orientation with multiple identified clients was not everyone's cup of tea. Here are a few additional thoughts about my foster family therapy experiences:

1. I experienced competent foster family systems and dysfunctional ones, just like nuclear and extended families. For the healthier systems, the work was about empowering, offering clinical advice and observations, and accessing support systems. Identifying, addressing, and reframing issues. My role was as a go between for clients, foster parents, doctors, social services, and other clinicians. For the dysfunctional systems, work was all the above plus addressing bio family and

1:1 issues. I think the homeostasis included foster child pathology as a detouring mechanism for the biological family dysfunction. I already discussed this, but I think it's important to mention it again. Foster mom's clinical affective symptoms, bio sibling issues, axis II symptoms, addiction. All masked by the bigger cans of worms provided by the foster kids. Looking back, I realize that being a foster child automatically locked that person into the role of the identified patient. How could it not? They were removed and placed for a reason.

Think about Carla and the continuity of services that were provided (individual, foster family therapy, bio family therapy, consults with her school.) This was one of the smoothest transitions I ever experienced, and part of it had to be due to continuity. Plus, I developed trusting relationships with major figure is in her life. I remember thinking that this was how it should be with every kid in foster care.

These days, you pick up the paper and read about tragedies in foster homes. You never hear the success rates, but that's not my point here. I wonder how a family therapist could intervene by providing real systems work. Very frustrating!

The AIDS/HIV chapter still blows my mind with the offshoots from one initial case. Talk about the butterfly effect. Everything I've learned in counseling was encapsulated in AIDS awareness. I still get requests for prevention groups or specific staff trainings rooted in that initial five-thousand-dollar grant. Trust and relationships.

The last thing I'd like to comment on is the importance of hanging in with those resistant, snail's pace clients. I have the luxury of being independent. No insurance companies or supervisors pressuring me or limiting my contact, role, or modalities of treatment. The way I look at it, my clients are hanging in with me and it's costing them money. Think about Rick (anger management group) and Donna. We put our heads together and formulated a treatment plan as best we could. That case had a sad ending, but the trust they showed for me and the effort both made make me a little weepy.

I'm always pleased but no longer shocked when a client or family makes a huge leap of progress. Sometimes it seemingly comes out of nowhere. Or during a treatment vacation. Or after we have terminated. Who can say why? But this is why having faith in the process is crucial to the joy of providing psychotherapy.

A FEW SUGGESTED READINGS
(AND SEVERAL DVDS)

- *Complete Mental Health* by John Ingram Walker
- *Rethinking Substance Abuse*, edited by William R. Miller and Kathleen M. Carroll
- *Doing Family Therapy* by Robert Taibbi
- *The Underground Guide to Teenage Sexuality* by Michael J. Basso
- When the Body Says No by Gabor Mate, MD
- *The Addicted Brain* (DVD), presented by Thad A. Polk
- *Harm Reduction in Substance Use and High Risk Behavior* by Patest Riley

I start with *Complete Mental Health*. I've reread this book from cover to cover every two or three years. I've urged clinicians in consultation groups and therapists in workshops to buy it. If I were a professor in psych, *Complete Mental Health* would be required reading. As the title suggests, it's a review of everything mental health, everything I see in home-based counseling and prevention groups. Affective disorders, axis II disorders, anxiety, addiction, autistic spectrum, meds, holistic techniques, neuro info, sleep disturbances, adolescence, aging concerns, diagnostic criteria, etc.

I especially like chapter eight, entitled "Understanding and Managing Somatoform and Factitious Disorders." This is murky stuff, and I need a frame of reference. (Is this a somatization disorder or an undifferentiated somatoform disorder?) His case studies help clarify the murkiness. Being a private and fairly isolated therapist in people's homes with individual, developmental, and systemic issues and symptoms zinging at me is daunting. I need to be able to focus and develop a practical working hypothesis.

At the end of each chapter, the author offers an assessment: "Are you an alcoholic?" "Are you depressed?" I may not literally use these assessments with my clients, but as a personal reference, they are a valuable tool. I need to be reminded because I can't remember everything. The clinicians quiz is exactly that, a review of each chapter's material.

I've referred to the author's cosmic humor, which I absolutely agree allows us to sort through trauma, craziness, sadness, and unusual stress without going bonkers ourselves. You should check out his "Bedlam Christmas Carols from Cyberspace" (page twenty-four) or "Mental Health Telephone Instructions from Cyberspace" (page twenty-five). Both are witty and instructional. I've always used humor in my work, which has not always been favorably received by other clinicians. This book not only normalizes it but encourages humor for all it can do.

Rethinking Substance Abuse is the first addiction and substance abuse book I read that made sense to me, based on my clinical experiences. First of all, it takes a harm reduction approach. Secondly, it takes systemic factors into account when diagnosing and treating addiction issues. Reading this book was a breath of fresh air. So much of what we have been told as kids, lay-people, and professionals is bullshit based on what's legal versus illegal, what has been funded for research or not, or supported by lobbyists (or not.) I give you the tobacco industry as an example. *Rethinking Substance Abuse* cuts through all of that with research and objectivity. And treatment suggestions from real experts. Each chapter finishes with robust principles, a summation of the major points. I appreciated chapter eleven, entitled "Family and Other Close Relationships," in which Barbara S. McGrady vividly describes what I see in my outreach cases as well as prevention and anger management groups. The final chapter (eighteen), "Drawing the Science Together," is authored by William R Miller and Kathleen M Carrol.

This chapter includes ten principles and ten treatment recommendations. Principles include drug use as a chosen behavior, drug problems emerging gradually along a continuum, the tendency of substance abuse to be self-perpetrating as well as motivation being a critical factor regarding both prevention and intervention.

Treatment implications include a shared responsibility by the public and private sectors, the need to understand drug issues in a wider life context, and the need to utilize positive reinforcement for nonuse.

That's just a sample of principles and recommendations. They reflect what I've seen for almost forty years, and I would bet that if you showed them to a room full of experienced substance abuse therapists, the reaction would be "That's what I'm talking about!" When I provide substance abuse workshops to any clinical staff, social workers, or teachers, I always include excerpts from *Rethinking Substance Abuse*. If I were teaching a course in this subject matter, this would be my number one reference.

Doing family therapy reinforces my belief in systems work, engaging with the family regardless of the identified patient's presenting issues/symptoms, and second-order change. This is real family therapy, not just supportive coaching for the parent who makes the call about their disturbed child. I especially cheer chapter four ("The Basic Seven") with basic suggestions for second order work. These include:

A) Determine the client and problem
B) Block dysfunctional pattern
C) Experience before explanation

When I'm working with a particularly challenging (crazy) family system, I review these principles. If I'm feeling useless and totally incompetent, this book reminds me that I've unbalanced a dysfunctional system, so people's anxiety—including my own—should increase. It's that homeostasis thing again.

Chapters eleven and twelve both address parent/adolescent struggles. When I read these chapters, it's deja vu all over again. The anxiety that I feel is a small sample of the huge anxiety created during the parent and child autonomy/dependency dance. Made worse in families with affective disorders, axis II symptoms, and addiction. Or all three! Doing family therapy normalizes that it's okay for me to feel a little freaked out.

Chapter sixteen ("Staying Sane-Survival Tips for Therapists") should be standard curriculum in graduate school. Supervision and training are obvious, but the "quick and easy: miscellaneous survival skills" are just as important.

Diversification, time awareness/control, taking vacations, and spending time with colleagues. All are common sense techniques for avoiding burnout. I would add regular exercise, a healthy diet, and regulated sleep. Nobody ever taught me this stuff. I learned by trial and error while watching other clinicians thrive or burn out bases on their own survival techniques. Doesn't this make total sense?

Michael J. Basso's *The Underground Guide to Teenage Sexuality* is based on questions students asked him when he taught health and sexuality. His book brings me back to my AIDS awareness program when I was bombarded with STI and sexuality questions from adults, teens, and latency-aged kids. I would urge anyone who does prevention work or sex ed to read this book. His explanations are straight forward, sensitive, and objective. The info (especially male and female anatomy) is substantial. This is another example of needing an accessible reference because I can't remember everything. Sometimes I bring *The Underground Guide...* to my prevention groups, hand it around, and have participants read excerpts that catch their eye. The ones who think they know everything always find something of interest. I especially like the chapters on HIV and STI, sexual anatomy, and contraception. Unless you've done sex ed and STI prevention with kids, you can't appreciate the scope of questions you get asked. This book has all those questions with thoughtful answers.

When the Body Says No is clearly the most controversial book on my short suggested reading list. It goes against traditional western/medical model thinking and views pathology from a mind and body holistic and environmentally triggered point of view. That title symbolizes the primary theme of the book: on a cellular and multi-generational level, your body's defense mechanisms (like your immune system) will compensate for trauma, being too selfless and compliant, and having lousy boundaries. Your body says no when you cannot! I think about this when I teach assertiveness or address codependency. The author relates this dynamic to all sorts of medical conditions, including blood sugar disorders, asthma, and cancer. I know this thinking freaks some people out, but I think he nails it.

Anyone who has ever worked with multi-problem families can attest to the interwoven nature of somatic/medical issues and trauma/affective/ substance related symptoms. This also relates to the genetic/environmental debate. Gabor Mate, throughout his book, sites multiple research studies linking chronic stress, trauma, and pathological caregiving to medical disorders. If you believe that the mind and body construct is actually one process with ongoing feedback, this is the book for you. Holistic techniques are also emphasized. Lower stress, eat a nutritious diet, exercise, and regulate sleep. Do whatever you have to do to regulate your body. Makes sense, right?

When the Body Says No includes a paragraph on page 243 that I would like to quote:

> No disease has a single cause. Even where significant risks can be identified—such as biological heredity in some autoimmune diseases or smoking and lung cancer—these vulnerabilities do not exist in isolation. Personality does not itself cause disease; one does not get cancer simply from repressing anger or ALS just from being too nice. A systems model recognizes that many processes and factors work together in the formation of disease or in the creation of health... According to the biopsychosocial view, individual biology reflects the history of a human organism in lifelong interaction with an environment, a perpetual interchange of energy in which psychological and social factors are as vital as physical ones...

Wow! That quote just about sums up what I deeply believe after thirty-five years of counseling. Disrupting homeostasis, second-order change, the butterfly effect, holistic techniques. Thank you, Gabor Mate for confirming what I've always felt in my guts but was told was wrong by traditional western thinking.

Which brings us to several DVDs on my list, *The Addicted Brain*, presented by Thad A. Polk. This program is offered by the Great Courses and is a tremendous resource for anybody who provides substance abuse counseling. The research is up to date, and Professor Polk presents his material in an engaging and straightforward manner. This course contains twelve lectures. The ones that I find the most helpful are:

#3 "How Addiction Hijacks the Brain"
#4 "Genetics—Born to be an Addict"

#7 "Alcohol-Social Lubricant or Drug of Abuse"
#8 "The Science of Marijuana"
#10 "The Science of Poppies, Pleasure, and Pain"
#12 "Junk Food, Porn, Video Games—Addictions."

These chapters all apply to my current caseload, whether it's individual adolescent referrals (weed dependency and gaming) male and female anger management groups (ETOH and opiates), interventions (ETOH, Opiates). The genetic component and addictive brain apply to all of the above. The science of poppies, pleasure, and pain and applies to the epidemic of heroin overdoses and deaths. There was a sense of karma while taking this course and getting deluged with overdose stories from anger management. And people need updated info on marijuana since it is now decriminalized legal or medically prescribed. I would suggest those interested to watch *The Addicted Brain* while reading *Rethinking Substance Abuse*, because they complement one another.

The next DVD is the *Science of Integrative Medicine*. The instructor is Brunt A. Bauer, MD. This is also offered by the Great Courses. This is exactly what the title says: a holistic and preventative approach to medical issues. I refer to Dr. Bauer's info in all my consulting work: anger management, family therapy, individual, sobriety, couples, teens. My anger management program includes one holistic class, and that includes *The Science of Integration Medicine* (nutrition, exercise, sleep, relation techniques) and *Blue Zones*. The latter is research into specific geographic areas that have the highest percentage of centenarians (people who live to 100). If you want to be impressed, I would suggest reading *Blue Zones* and watching Dr. Bauer's course. Both confirm my core beliefs for overall health.

Another DVD from the Great Courses I would highly recommend is *Mind-Body Medicine: Harm Reduction*. I've always used a harm reduction approach as well as an abstinence approach for addiction and dependency issues. The abstinence approach is for extreme or life-threatening situations. This book reinforces my belief in the former. How about this forward from Nick Crofts:

> We are a dependent society that has self-medicated with drugs
> and alcohol forever! This is self-perpetuating and moneymaking.

Think alcohol, nicotine products, and pharmaceuticals. It's probably never going to go away. So we have to learn to manage it with healthier coping mechanisms. This book is a great tool for going forward.